OBJECTIONS TO HUMANISM

FOLLOWING the publication of *Objections to Christian Belief*, one reviewer wrote: "The obvious next step . . . would be for a group of intellectual non-believers to write with equal harshness about the contradictions or inadequacies of their own beliefs".

Four leading humanists here take up that challenge. Just as Christianity was put in the dock by Christians, now humanism is examined by humanists in the same spirit of ruthless self-analysis. Indeed, this is probably the first time that humanists have ever been openly self-critical.

The editor, Director of the newly formed British Humanist Association, introduces the volume by stating what the essentials of humanism are. Professor Hepburn criticizes attempts of humanists to reconstruct humanism on a religious basis. Kathleen Nott deals with the aridity of mere rationalism, Kingsley Martin with the rejection of Utopianism and disenchantment with the idea of progress. The editor's concluding essay faces what must, for most people, be the most emotional objection to humanism—'the pointlessness of it all' if humanists *are* right.

Anyone set thinking by the present controversy raging around *Honest to God*, *Soundings*, and *Objections to Christian Belief*—will find this a stimulating and authoritative introduction to a way of thinking which has a long tradition and a growing influence.

OBJECTIONS
TO
HUMANISM

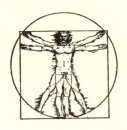

H. J. Blackham
Professor Ronald Hepburn
Kingsley Martin
Kathleen Nott

Edited by H. J. Blackham

GREENWOOD PRESS, PUBLISHERS
WESTPORT, CONNECTICUT

BL
2747.6
B55
1974

Library of Congress Cataloging in Publication Data

Blackham, Harold John, 1903–
    Objections to humanism.

    Reprint of the 1963 ed. published by Constable,
London.
    1. Humanism. I. Title.
[BL2747.6.B55 1974]   211'.6   73-16796
ISBN 0-8371-7235-7

First published in 1963 by Constable, London

Reprinted with the permission of Constable Publishers

Reprinted in 1974 by Greenwood Press,
a division of Williamhouse-Regency Inc.

Library of Congress Catalog Card Number 73-16796

ISBN 0-8371-7235-7

Printed in the United States of America

CONTENTS

Humanism : The Subject of the Objections

H. J. BLACKHAM

Classical Humanism

'The proper study of mankind is man.'

POPE'S well-worn line expressed a hard-won conclusion and a modern starting-point. 'The Enlightenment', says Ernst Cassirer, 'gradually learned to do without the "absolute" in the strictly metaphysical sense, without the ideal of "God-like knowledge". Instead appears a purely human ideal which the age seeks to define and to realize with increasing precision and rigour.' (*The Philosophy of the Enlightenment*, p. 354.) With crudeness and vigour Hume showed emphatic satisfaction at the rout of 'the whole train of monkish virtues', a more popular manifestation of the humanism of the age than abandonment of the ideal of 'God-like knowledge' enthroned by Plato and Aristotle.

Celibacy, fasting, penance, mortification, self-denial, humility, silence, solitude, and the whole train of monkish virtues; for what reason are they everywhere rejected by men of sense, but because they serve to no manner of purpose; neither advance a man's fortune in the world, nor render him a more valuable member of society; neither qualify him for the entertainment of company, nor increase his power of self-enjoyment? We observe, on the contrary, that they cross all these desirable ends; stupefy the understanding and harden the heart, obscure the fancy and sour the temper. We justly, therefore, transfer them to the opposite column, and place them in the catalogue of vices; nor has any superstition force sufficient among men of the world, to pervert entirely these natural sentiments. A gloomy hare-brained enthusiast, after his death, may have a place in the calendar; but will scarcely ever be admitted, when alive, into intimacy and society, except by those who are as delirious and dismal as himself. (*An Enquiry into the Principles of Morals*, sect. ix, part i, para. 219.)

The abandonment of theological preoccupations for a concentration on the finite and the exploration of it in all directions carried on the enterprise of the Renaissance:

Humanism is the effort of men to think, to feel, and to act for themselves, and to abide

8

by the logic of results. This attitude of spirit is common to all the varied energies of Renaissance life. Brunelleschi, Macchiavelli, Michael Angelo, Cesare Borgia, Galileo, are here essentially at one. In each case a new method is suddenly apprehended, tested, and carried firmly to its conclusion. Authority, habit, orthodoxy, are disregarded or defied. The argument is pragmatic, realistic, human. The question, "Has this new thing a value?" is decided directly by the individual in the court of his experience; and there is no appeal. That is good which is seen to satisfy the human test, and to have brought an enlargement of human power. (*The Architecture of Humanism* by Geoffrey Scott, p. 191. London: Constable, reprinted 1947.)

But the confidence and purpose of the Enlightenment were founded on the modern empiricism of Newton and Locke, confirmed in 'the century of genius' by spectacular success in achieving progressive knowledge. With the excitement of this first explosion of knowledge went a new enthusiasm for society, both in its genial aspect and in its powerful role as the moulder of human behaviour and the source of the arts and sciences and all human resources: because society conditions good and evil, man can become in the ethical sense his own creator.

This Promethean vision of civilization, which Matthew Arnold defined later as 'the humanization of man in society', makes the Enlightenment the golden age of humanism. There has followed a growing disillusionment: with the

9

social consequences of science, with the fruits of democracy, with organized society and its powers, with human values and their sufficiency. 'Freedom', 'tolerance', 'progress', sacred words of the Enlightenment, have become dirty words in some quarters (MRA, for instance), and nowhere evoke the enthusiasm and inspire the vision of the humanist dawn. Yet the passionate humanism of Diderot or Condorcet remains an enviable folly to the humanist of today, if folly it was, for we find it harder to rise above the contemptible and ephemeral of our own time, the blocks and diversions, the catastrophic trends, to the level of a steady view of the ascent of humanity. All the same, we are in a better position actually to achieve what they dreamed of, for we are in a position to take the measure of the problem, and it is the real that is rich in unworked resources: the ideal is as insubstantial as light.

Humanists hope to learn from experience, and they have not abandoned this hope for a return to the faith of their fathers, which they think is a counsel of despair.

Carl Becker, a hostile but amusing witness in the modern case against the humanists of the Enlightenment, says that they were incapable of learning from experience since they were out to prove their faith in a revealed body of knowledge, like medieval scholastics. He goes on to formulate the essential articles of their religion thus:

(1) man is not natively depraved; (2) the end of life is life itself, the good life on earth instead of the beatific life after death; (3) man is capable, guided solely by the light of reason

and experience, of perfecting the good life on earth; and (4) the first and essential condition of the good life on earth is the freeing of men's minds from the bonds of ignorance and superstition, and of their bodies from the arbitrary oppression of the constituted social authorities.' (*The Heavenly City of the Eighteenth Century Philosophers*, p. 102.)

Stated thus, these beliefs are denials of orthodox Christian beliefs by affirmation of their contraries; and the unkind critic who states them thus ridicules those who professed them, because, he says, whilst thinking themselves enlightened and emancipated from religious superstitions they were zealots of a more arbitrary secular faith. Nevertheless, modern humanists need not disavow these beliefs of their predecessors. 'Past times are as if they had never been. It is always necessary to start at the point at which one already stands, and at which nations have arrived' (Voltaire). It would be more positive and more just to recognize the permanent roots of humanism in two related fundamental quests of universal import: free inquiry and social agreement.

Free Inquiry

Free inquiry, *libre examen*, may be caricatured in the spirit of Carl Becker as a secular version of the Protestant 'priesthood of all believers': it is better thought of as a more general principle, that each must think and decide for himself on important questions concerning the life he has and his conduct of it; and, most general, that nothing is exempt from human question. This means that there is no immemorial tradition, no revelation, no authority, no privileged knowledge (first principles, intuitions, axioms) which is beyond question because beyond experience and which can be used as a standard by which to interpret experience. There is only experience to be interpreted in the light of further experience, the sole source of all standards of reason and value, for ever open to question. This radical assumption is itself, of course, open to question, and stands only in so far as it is upheld by experience.

Free inquiry is radical and dangerous, and may seem to threaten the undoing of man, for, as Burke observed, no human institution, nothing, however sacred, not God himself, can stand against it. Even Auguste Comte, positivist and agnostic, thought that this, the Protestant principle and the principle of the *philosophes*, was radical mischief, since it could produce nothing but anarchy and dissolution, and made order and progress impossible. Science, he thought, told men what to think, with no nonsense about it.

Therefore humanists, who do not put anything beyond question, have to meet these fears and the real dangers they bespeak. They do so by underlining the *discipline* of free inquiry, and by linking this quest with the related quest for social agreement.

Free inquiry is not irresponsible thinking; on the contrary, in so far as it is methodical and systematic, it has established agreement and its own tradition, that is to say, its own criteria and system of control. This does not mean that organized inquiry, science, is either free from cults of opinion, sects, errors, fashions, or that, being free inquiry, it is itself beyond question. It

gives rise to many questions, and the philosophy
of science is the business of raising such questions.
Just because the validity of science itself remains
always open to question and because its results
remain always subject to falsification by further
experience, this provisional, corrigible, progressive knowledge is the standard of attainable
certainty and reliability. Only in so far as
science really is organized free inquiry is it a
humanist quest, and not secular dogmatism.

There is a second sense in which science may
be both positive and open. 'Science' is an abstract
term for the particular sciences engaged in
special fields of investigation. None of these
sciences is dealing with questions on which the
historical religions have made their declarations;
none, for example, is employing and testing the
God-idea as an hypothesis in any investigation
of natural phenomena. Does this mean that
science has no bearing on the ultimate questions
raised by theology? If so, it would relegate such
questions to the ancient world of inconclusive
verbal argumentation about and about in the
closed circuit of dogmatic, sceptic, fideistic, or
eclectic positions which minds could argue
themselves into and out of with equal facility.
Science does have no direct bearing on these
questions, since it is not dealing with them, but
it does have a far-reaching indirect bearing,
since it is the type of attainable knowledge and
any question which is not amenable to scientific
handling is itself put in question.

Scientific inquiry presupposes the situation of
human beings confronting objects in this world.
Anything supposed outside these conditions is

13

not open to its inquiry. Anything totally transcendent, encompassing both subject and object,
for example, is beyond such an inquiry, and
beyond conceptual thought. Science explores and
tries to find an order in what is totally given. It
has no means and no hope of saying why what is
is as it is, nor why there should be something and
not nothing. The assumption that conceptual
thought has the run of the cosmos, so to speak,
is gratuitous. Ultimately, everything as given is
equally inscrutable and mysterious; there is
nothing privileged in terms of which all the rest
can be explained. This is what is meant by the
renunciation of 'God-like knowledge'. A-Gnosti-
cism, which is more fundamental and radical
than atheism, is the only position warranted by
experience: recognition of the permanent nature
and conditions of human knowledge, with its open
horizon of continuous progressive investigation.

'Agnosticism', which is simply and solely the
word for a disclaimer, a renunciation of both
affirmations and denials about what lies outside
the reach of human thought, is usually treated in
practice as the ground for a virtual atheism, as by
the Victorian agnostics, or for a virtual theism, as
(in different ways) by Jaspers, Marcel, and Buber.
It is a counsel of perfection to say that this is
indefensible, for one has to come to a practical
conclusion in order to live. Nevertheless, in all
rigour, agnosticism is the only defensible position,
and it does not advance anybody one step on the
road to atheism nor one step on the road to
theism. Progress is to be made only along the
many paths followed by the investigations of
empirical science. This is not progress on the road

14

to 'God-like knowledge'. All the same, a philosophical interest in the findings of the sciences,
following the same empirical clue, 'Nature is her
own standard, one thing throws light on another',
can attempt to discern a world order and piece
together a coherent world picture; which will
tend to establish 'a reasonably grounded natural
theology', as Mr Bezzant hopes and believes
(*Objections to Christian Belief*, p. 109), or to confirm
the non-teleological assumption of humanists,
that the universe taken as a whole does not show
evidence of design.

The abandonment of Gnosticism, of human
claims to 'God-like knowledge', is not in itself a
rejection of the Christian claim to Revelation.
That claim has to be examined on its own
evidence. In *Objections to Christian Belief*, Dr
Vidler and Mr Bezzant reasonably complain that
modern secular man is simply not interested, and
makes up his mind against the Christian claim
without giving it a serious hearing. This objection
would lie against the humanism of anyone who had
not taken into account the crucial considerations.
But what are the crucial considerations? There is
the preaching of the gospel by them of old time,
and there is the exemplary examination of
objections to the gospel by these teachers of
today. The appeal ultimately is to the man
within: 'What think ye of Christ?' And this
biblical question should be supplemented by:
'How do you respond to the community of
believers?' For good or ill, and for whatever reasons
and motives, humanists are among those who have
not been able to answer such questions in a way
that would number them with the Christians.

Social Agreement

Only too obviously, there is precious little agreement in the world outside the province of the natural sciences—and perhaps less inside than is popularly supposed. Nevertheless, agreement is the ultimate criterion for values as well as for facts, some humanists would hold, and at any rate for rules which concern everybody in a society. Human beings become human in being socialized, and society is instituted in the rules, customs, procedures by which conduct is regulated and co-operation secured, facilitated, and maintained. If I am party to the rules they are binding on me and I am responsible for upholding and enforcing them on other parties as well as for conforming to them. The rules, except those that are merely conventions like the Highway Code, cannot be wholly agreed, since they are necessarily compromises, but as compromises they are agreed, and if they remain open to question and revision because agreed procedures are provided by means of which to put them in question and try to obtain revision, they are meanwhile binding. That is, the rules are binding in so far as they are provisional, as scientific propositions are certain in so far as they are provisional. This positive correlation of certainty and obligation with the provisional character of propositions and rules, and the corresponding refusal to accept absolute claims is characteristic of humanist thinking.

But this democratic social order is independent of ultimate (and contentious) beliefs, Christian, humanist, or other. The simple point here is that

16

we cannot, as in the old Christendom, make ultimate beliefs, nor unbelief, the ground of our social morality, and we do not need to do so; for the kind of agreement that is needed for living together is an agreement about conventions (like the Highway Code), procedures (like parliamentary government), rights (like civil liberties), and mutual expectations (from common honesty to neighbour help). Upon this common foundation of social order and co-operation, different ultimate beliefs governing different ideals of life and styles of living may co-exist in equal security. Not only is such a common social foundation good for order, it is also good for the productive co-operation which furnishes means and multiplies opportunity, in a word, creates that practicability of purpose for all which is the concrete content of freedom.

In this matter there is no necessary difference between humanists and Christians, since the social foundation in question is independent of ultimate beliefs and secures and serves all alike. In practice, however, there is this difference, that all humanists want to see a consensus of the secular *foundations* of society fully prevail, whereas some, perhaps most, Christians insist that 'this is a Christian country, and . . . its moral standards are founded in a Christian tradition accepted by nearly everyone, if often tacitly' (the Pilkington Committee). Only an acknowledged distinction between the social ground of morality and the personal (or group) superstructures on that basis can reconcile the claims of all—Christians, humanists, and others.

Human Values

There is no room here to elaborate the differences between Christian and humanist morals. They are more radical and far-reaching than is usually recognized or acknowledged. Perhaps 'the whole train of monkish virtues' is dubious now to many Christians. Perhaps many feel with Professor MacKinnon that the duty of sacrifice can be mistakenly and dangerously over-emphasized, and that the characteristically humanist tests of utility and pleasure are applicable to any sane ethics (*Objections to Christian Belief*, pp. 24–5, 28–9). But the Christian must remain concentrated upon and bound by the example of Christ as the supreme model for human living. Now Christ as a human personality is an enigma, but as a standard and pattern there is no doubt nor obscurity about him: he is the archetype of unqualified submission and obedience to the will of God, the God of Abraham and of Isaac and of Jacob. It is impossible to follow Christ on any other terms, and the humanist finds acceptance of these terms a violation of himself and his whole experience. His rejection of Christ is therefore categorical: he can do no other. There is no separation of Christian ethics from the particular faith of which Christ is the supreme exemplar.

There is no supreme exemplar of humanist ethics, because, on humanist assumptions, there is no *summum bonum*, no chief end of all action, no far-off crowning event to which all things move and for which all things exist, no teleology, no definitive human nature even. Instead, there are many possibilities, better and worse, and ways of avoiding the worse and realizing and increasing the better. Thus there are many patterns of good living, which can be exemplified, and none that is best or comprehensively or exhaustively good. As Cicero pointed out, Ajax, Ulysses, and Cato were different persons and they lived and acted in character; what was right and proper for one to do was not necessarily so for the others, even in the same circumstances, Cato's suicide, for example. 'The thought that virtue is a *natural* excellence, the ideal expression of human life, has not impressed Jews, Christians, nor Moslems, any more than it impressed the vehement barbarian Israelites who were their ancestors and masters' (Santayana). Virtue as one's own excellence, however, would be a misleading statement of humanist ethics unless it were understood to include 'the most material part of virtue', as Hume called it, 'public spirit, or a regard to the community'. For this ground-work of public order and co-operation is the condition of all good possibilities. That is why Cicero reproached the philosophers and others who contracted out of or thought they were above the battle; it was their duty not only not to do injustice, but also to join in ensuring that it was not done. Those who preferred the life of service to the life of pleasure or contemplation belonged to mankind. Hercules and Prometheus were the exemplars for these, and they had earned the gratitude of mankind.

Therefore, although hedonism or the pleasure principle has been important in humanist ethics, it is stressed because of the evil consequences of neglecting it, not really because it is the sole criterion. After all, only the religions encourage people to hope to convert all experience into permanent enjoyment. In this world, a single ethical criterion is never adequate. There is always a balance of considerations, to be weighed in the light of experience.

Both purpose and hospitality, drive and openness, initiative and waiting, are needed if one is to win from life its greatness. As spectator and actor, one stands in the midst of abundance, an excess of values, if one is both purposive and responsive. But these values are human, temporal, perishable; so most humanists think. What of it? Some find in achievement consolation against the enigma of fate. T. H. Huxley in 1893 ended his Romanes Lecture: 'So far, we all may strive in one faith towards one hope:

> It may be that the gulfs will wash us down,
> It may be we shall touch the Happy Isles
> . . . but something ere the end,
> Some work of noble note may yet be done.'

Others remember that what time bears away is born of time. Those who reject the humanist rejection of the absolute know not what they do. They want their flowers in wax or in flame; but these are not flowers.

Tolerance

Clearly, tolerance is required by the kind of social agnosticism which would exclude ultimate beliefs from the consensus which holds society together. And tolerance has been a characteristic humanist virtue, neither as a social lubricant nor as a tactical expedient, but because it expresses the permanent truth of the human condition. 'What is tolerance?' asks Voltaire. 'It belongs to humanity. We are all formed of weaknesses and errors; let us mutually pardon each other's follies, it is the first law of nature.' How ironical that Palmiro Togliatti, secretary of the Italian Communist Party, in a Preface to a party reproduction of Voltaire's *Treatise on Toleration* in 1949, should have treated Voltaire's line as party tactics in the situation of the time. By all means let the struggle for men's minds and hearts go on, by all fair and peaceful means, but let it be remembered that the renunciation of all other means, like the Golden Rule itself, is a matter of social agreement; and this is a condition that has to be worked for.

There has been a scholarly kind of humanism which makes an ideal of the play of free-ranging disinterested intelligence. Terence's line gives general expression to this: 'I am a man; nothing of human interest is not of interest to me'. Sartre has said that three generations of Frenchmen were bred in such a humanism of universal sympathies, with the result that they had no knowledge of evil, and therefore no standard by which to judge Nazism, no motive to halt it. This is a difficult world; like the innocence of philosophers and contemplatives, relativist principles can work evil as do absolutes and the doers of injustice. But there is no need. Humanists are called to be actors as well as spectators, and the mere principle of bringing every relevant consideration into the reckoning, the systematic appeal to experience, should correct one-sidedness.

All the same, the humanism of the spectator

may be justified in his own case. Santayana is an example. He was disorientated in youth and remained not at home in the world, all the more free to travel and stay wherever he had a mind or an opportunity, never expecting to find, never seeking, a home. This bred out of a convinced materialist an invincible platonist, a spectator of all time and of all existence, a seasoned witness and judge, who might be also a victim but could never be disillusioned, because he had shifted the centre of his life and his interest from the will to the imagination. This was a vocation to which he dedicated himself early and in which he remained faithful. He always overcame the rash impulse to claim an absolute rightness for what he preferred, and his choice deserves no reproach. In any case, it is no mean choice to eschew miscellaneous living and cultivate a rational life in view of the truth. For Santayana, any choice was but one possibility, and the great question was, what perfection have you achieved on the basis of your choice?

The question of humanist commitment is fundamental and not quite simple, but first, and briefly, some other questions.

Some Questions

Surely, all that has been said shows how sophisticated a position humanism is, suitable only for intellectuals, unintelligible and un-attainable to simple people? Not at all. On the contrary, the simplest people will for themselves think that we don't know and can't know about ultimate things, that ethics are much the most important and certain part of the great religions and say much the same in all of them, that if you don't know the difference between right and wrong the parson can't tell you, that we should respect other people's convictions and way of life, that the Bible should be judged by common sense and moral sense, that it is reasonable to co-operate in a society which is regulated to serve the interests of all and not merely of a few or of some, that this is the only life we are sure of and we better make the most of it. These simplicities are more evident to the simple than to the sophisticated, for whom they raise many questions. Humanism is a defence of this popular simplicity, as well as a defence of more complex forms of the same outlook.

Is humanism a philosophy? Two professional philosophers who are humanists differ on this. Professor Nowell Smith, writing in a humanist journal, quotes Dr Corliss Lamont of the American Humanist Association: 'Naturalistic humanism challenges men to rely on their own intelligence, courage, and effort in building their happiness and fashioning their destiny in this world of infinite possibilities'. He goes on to say that he accepts this as a correct account of what humanism is and that he concurs wholly in the attitude expressed, but he as strongly disagrees with Lamont's contention that 'humanism stands in need of a sound metaphysics'. Humanists take sides, he says, on the big metaphysical issue of design or purpose in the universe taken as a whole, and some humanists are philosophers in the sense that they have the training and skill to justify, present, and defend their views and to discuss metaphysical issues, and many (hopefully most) humanists will want to think out and discuss what is meant by and involved in the kind of position and programme indicated in Dr Lamont's statement; but humanists do not stand in need of, nor to gain from, an agreed humanist metaphysics. Indeed, it is not too much to say that such a metaphysics would be the death of humanism, as any orthodoxy is the death of philosophy. Humanism is a philosophical position and needs a philosophical defence, but it is not 'a philosophy'.

Is humanism a religion? Again disagreement. Is it about a word? Historically, humanist movements have clashed with religion. This was true of the Epicureans, the *philosophes*, and the Utilitarians. But the clash in these cases was something like a clash of sects, and some of these humanists, for example, Epicurus or James Mill, exemplified the very type of the religious man. Bentham was aware of introducing a new type of humanity and a new religion. 'Benthamite? What sort of animal is that? . . . to be sure a new religion would be an odd sort of thing without a name: accordingly there ought to be one for it . . . *Utilitarian* . . . would be the *mot propre*.' But the spirit of humanism is in rebellion against the narrow horizons of cults and sects, whether within or outside orthodox faith. Thus the Enlightenment takes up and expands Renaissance humanism, and Diderot speaks for this enlarged view: 'Men have banished the Deity; they have relegated it to a sanctuary; the walls of a temple limit its view; it does not exist outside. Madmen that you are! destroy these circles which restrict your ideas; set God free; see him everywhere where he is, or say that he does not exist at all.'

24

This is the leaven of the humanist spirit whether
working within a faith or outside all religious
faiths. What is important is not that humanism
shall or shall not be called a religion, but that it
shall not become sectarian.

Although humanism is certainly offered as a
guide to the conduct of human life, a view and a
way, a basis of union and action, a commitment,
and these words have rather a religious tone,
there are good reasons why it should not be
called a religion. Humanists do not normally
preserve age-old religious categories in their
thinking (numinous, holy, sacred, absolute, transcendent, divine) and modernize their contents.
This does not necessarily mean, I think, that they
exclude a whole dimension from their lives, that
they are deficient in the sixth sense which religious
people have. Indeed, acceptance of the religious
categories may make one insensitive here, for it is
precisely in a questioning approach to the world,
in an openness that sits loose to all categories and
handles instrumentally all ideas and ideals, that
the humanist quest is pursued; and the attitudes
and responses which are formed in this way are
not to be prefabricated. To become a religion, as
to become a philosophy, would be the death of
humanism. What we really do make of this
world in which we find ourselves is not likely to
differ in all respects from what others have made
of it and will make of it, but there is all the
difference in the world between what we do
really make of it and unquestionable attitudes
which may be taken over instead. Perhaps the
characteristic note of humanism is unworldly
worldliness, impassioned materialism.

Thus it might be said that humanists aspire to be simple with the simplest and to be more philosophical than the schools and more religious than the sects, and one might go on to say more political than the parties. For to the question, is humanism political, the answer is again that political institutions and parties, like ideas and ideals, are instrumental. Political action aims at legislation, and takes effect mainly in laws. But laws are a beginning only, a set of new possibilities, and humanism as social action begins with the laws as they are, and sees what can be realized within them, by means of them, and in spite of them, and what legislative changes are needed or desirable. Humanism in action is not a political party nor a lobby nor any kind of specialized association, nor is it related to these social instruments in the same way as a church, which, after all, is a kind of specialized association. Organized humanism is a general association with no *specific* object, a fellowship in shared general assumptions and shared general aims which are life-shaping and world-shaping in tendency, a shared general responsibility.

Humanist Commitment

What do you do? is the last question here, and the first challenge of the impatient inquirer. To be a Christian, says Montaigne, is to be more than ordinarily just, charitable, kind. In practice this may be so, and one might say that in practice to be a humanist is to be more than ordinarily honest-minded, public-spirited, tolerant. It doesn't sound as nice, but the comparison in practice would probably yield fairly equal marks, and, anyhow, the words would have to be spelled out before comment is profitable. But faith without works is not Christianity, and unbelief without any effort to help shoulder the consequences for mankind is not humanism. If one wakes up from a sense of unlimited dependence to a supposed independence, instead of unlimited interdependence, it is simply to change illusions, for the worse.

Unlimited shared responsibility for creating the conditions for all of a life worthy to be called human, a human providence, is the colossal undertaking to be shouldered by man without God. Men face together the common problems of mankind, the classical evils of ignorance, poverty, and disease, the spectre of insecurity, the characteristic weaknesses of human beings, the population nightmare; on their side they have the arts and sciences and the vast resources of social co-operation. Humanists are simple-minded enough to think that the common sense of the situation calls for an attack on these problems with the aid of these resources, and that this has urgency and priority over the many and important differences which parcel out mankind in races, nations, classes, creeds, and other portions of total humanity. Of course this is simple-minded, but those versed in the history of religions know that only simpletons were ever inspired by simple truths, for everybody else is content to know they won't work.

Without some response to this call, without voluntary enlistment in the human enterprise, without something of a Promethean spirit, there is no humanism worth speaking about, for humanism is more a passion than an intellectual position. People who call themselves humanists, or don't, respond according to their sense of the task and its urgency, according to their capacities and opportunities, according to their willingness to serve, according to their hopes or fears for mankind; some with little more than goodwill, some few, a Diderot, a Condorcet, magnificently, generously, at full stretch, with enthusiasm. Enthusiasm for what? Not a vapid, effusive out-pouring; a sure-fingered outreaching after a visible ideal: enthusiasm for a fine quality of living, kindled in the lived life. Matthew Arnold's choice spirits drawn from all classes, generous and humane souls, lovers of man's perfection, who devote themselves to education and the public service are humanists in this profound sense.

Humanism in the stricter sense is justified by its production in every generation of its quota of just men. If one looks round amongst declared humanists living today and takes the liberty of naming Bertrand Russell and Julian Huxley and Barbara Wootton and Jean-Paul Sartre, and looks back at those recently dead and names Gilbert Murray and M. N. Roy and John Dewey, these are not merely the names of men of great gifts and achievements, they are the names of many-sided human beings of more than ordinary candour and public spirit who have lived and spent themselves in the human cause. You may find as many faults with them as you like, with their thinking, with their judgements, with their lives: they remain grand exemplars of what it means to be human, and to have one's passions and ends and values illumined by humanist thinking.

A Critique

of

Humanist

Theology

RONALD W. HEPBURN

TO argue against the Christian theologians is itself to do a kind of theology; and in this sense at
least many humanists are theologians part-time.
Occasionally, however, a humanist ventures on a
more ambitious theological task—a constructive,
or reconstructive, task. How much, he asks, can
be salvaged from the ruins (as he sees it) of the
traditional faiths: what do they contain that is
both humanly valuable and consistent with a
naturalistic view of the world? How can the
superstitious be sifted from the reasonable and the
illuminating? "What the world now needs",
writes Sir Julian Huxley, "is not merely a
rationalist denial of the old but a religious

affirmation of something new" (*The Humanist Frame* (1961), p. 41).

Here is a fascinating and immensely difficult project. How well is it being done? Those who accuse Christian apologists of slipshod thinking—they may properly be asked, how careful is their own?

Certainly on its *critical* side, humanist theology has been of widely varying merit. Christians have been entitled to complain that humanists have often worked with crude notions of transcendence (God as the celestial managing-director, or the ghost in the cosmic machine), and with even cruder ideas of religious psychology (e.g. all religion as motivated by fear). Today's humanist, however, is not usually a slapdash caricaturist of religion. Although he has by no means produced it unaided, there exists now a good deal of fairly scrupulous critical writing. My impression of the reconstructive work, on the other hand, is that much of it is not nearly so careful or alert to pitfalls as it needs to be. Humanist, naturalist religion is in need of a critique, and this essay will try to adumbrate one.

But first: why try to reconstruct at all? It must seem a pointless project to anyone who sees the strength of humanist thinking in its thorough-going secularism. Those whom the project attracts are people whose best, most momentous, experiences have been in some sense religious experiences, yet who are no more able than their happily secularist neighbour to interpret these experiences in the manner of the historical faiths. They wish to discover, naturally enough, what religious attitudes, evaluations, questings can remain available outside those faiths.

'*Nothing* remains available, for there can be no religion without the supernatural.' This is a possible answer—not, I think, a correct one. 'A very great deal remains available' is a second answer. 'Once jettison the transcendent, and religion is at last emancipated: a new and glorious phase in its development has begun.' This answer is exhilarating: but maybe premature, over-optimistic. It is easy to be intoxicated by the prospect of having one's agnosticism and religion too. To counteract this, one needs at every stage to ask, in the presence of religious language, is this language leading me to have well-grounded or ill-grounded hopes and expectations? Is it encouraging me to adopt attitudes that are really legitimate or illegitimate, rational or irrational, given my basic set of beliefs about man and the world? Is it spell-binding me—as it is well able to do—to confuse dream with reality, wishing with having?

'But the whole project is broken-backed', protests the radical critic of reconstructions. 'The object of worship and adoration was, and could only be, God. If we are right that God does not exist, no other object can properly take his place.'

The reconstructor should not lose heart. Recent philosophical studies of theism have not been so much concerned with evidence for or against God's existence, as with the question of the coherence or incoherence of the concept of God. If the concept is ultimately incoherent, that is because theism tries to pack into it a wealth of sublime but incompatible elements—God is personal but infinite, is in causal contact with the world but not in space and time, is impenetrably mysterious yet known beyond doubt in the Christian revelation. This is a downfall through excessive riches, and the non-theist should be encouraged to inquire whether some of the strands (which refuse to lie down together as elements of one deity) can function individually as foci of religious aspiration.

This sounds vaguely reasonable, it may be said, so long as it is kept reasonably vague. But what *are* these transferable elements, and can they really be counted on to retain their full numinous charge when redistributed about the unbeliever's universe? The element of "mystery" can serve as an example. "Science", writes Sir Julian Huxley, ". . . confronts us with a basic and universal mystery—the mystery of existence in general, and . . . of mind in particular. Why does the world exist? Why is the world-stuff what it is? . . . We do not know." This world can present itself as "alien and even hostile to human aspiration": yet we must learn to accept it as "the one basic mystery", to see it as furnishing a "background of reverence and awe" and fostering a "sense of wonder, strangeness and challenge" (*Ibid.*, p. 42). In some "reconstructions" the language of numinous awe is used to express a response to the tasks, revelations and necessary limits of science.

There may well be points of analogy—notable points; yet we must emphasize the enormous differences between these responses and responses signalled by this same vocabulary within, say,

32

Judaism or Christianity. We are far from the shudder and thrill of Job's or Isaiah's encounter with Jahweh, or the climax of the Passion narrative. The experience of mystery in the biblical cases is an amazed sense of being over-whelmed by something quite incomprehensible to us, but which presses in upon us clamantly: an active, holy mystery, not the inert mystery of an encompassing ignorance. If we call our response to the law-discovering work of science 'numinous awe', let us measure the distance between this new use of the phrase and its original use to mark the impact of a dramatic theophany, a theophany that defies law and annihilates thought. We are celebrating quite a different mystery: and mysteries are not always interchangeable.

Surely the reconstructors are well aware that these mysteries are different? Of course they are aware. Huxley states that the new religious vision will have "a totally different view of the mys-terious" (*Ibid., loc. cit.*). Yet he does want it still to retain crucial features of the old views. We are not to respond with repugnance or dismay but with awe and reverence and wonder. These are responses of undoubted human value and we should certainly *want* to find room for them in any religious reconstruction. But does the fact of our ignorance about why the world exists give us a really stable grounding for those responses? I doubt it. Some philosophers will even argue that there is no meaning in the question 'Why does anything exist?'; since they cannot conceive what *kind* of answer could logically be in order. If they are correct, no one response is better grounded than another.

33

Supposing one does not take that strong line: one may ask, why should I revere the unknowable? Reverence is for the morally great; it acknowledges dignity and worth. But here is a world "in many of its aspects . . . alien and even hostile to human aspiration". Are its unknowable aspects likely to be any *less* ambivalent? This time we do have a self-rejecting question!

It is tempting to say, therefore, that the humanist lacks an adequate or appropriate object of reverence and awe, still more an object of *numinous* awe. To retain the religious terms is not, dependably, to retain the substance and the experience. There is truth in this, but it is not the last word. The relation between 'religious experience' and 'object' is an extraordinarily and curiously complex one. It does not seem possible to pair off in any straightforward way beliefs about the object of religious concern with particular experiences legitimized by those beliefs. The slipperiness of this relation is what I wish to make the chief moral of this first section. It is an embarrassment both for the reconstructor and his critic.

For example, there are points of view from which the necessary limits of our knowledge seem not awesome but exasperating. There are ways of reflecting on the endlessness of the series of causes and effects, backwards or forwards in time, or indeed on the succession of moments of time themselves, that make these appear simply dull, tedious, irrelevant. And yet the most subtle shift of perspective can make those same reflections excitingly mysterious and religiously significant—can cause us to see our lives against a strange, unfamiliar and disturbing backcloth that both humiliates and enhances them. As if this were not perplexing enough, consider the case of mystical experience. Certain of the most intense and momentous of these seem not to be generated by any reflection or perception or entertaining of beliefs, or consciousness of an 'object' at all: but involve, rather, an emptying of content from the mind, even a blurring of the very distinction between subject and object.

II

So far we have been thinking of particular religious experiences, of mystery or awe, and the situations that may evoke them. More elaborate projects, however, for a 'common faith', an 'empiricist religion', a 'humanist religious frame-work' have in fact been worked out by humanists and other naturalists. We need to look at certain of these.[1]

First: some have claimed that the only proper religious goal, the worthiest object of aspiration and reverence, is a unified vision of our actual ideals, imaginatively expressed, perhaps in myth or in parables, or in more literal ways. Other reconstructors refuse to identify the object of highest unconditional regard with anything now conceivable. Since they see our ideals as always in course of development, they identify it rather with an unimaginable ultimate transformation

[1] There is room here only to give a schematic outline of some possible and plausible views rather than well-documented actual specimens. I should also state that not all the views alluded to are the work of authors who explicitly call themselves 'humanists'. What they share is the desire to construct an empirically or naturalistically based religion.

of these ideals. They may use a metaphor from mathematics and speak of the goal as a 'limit' to the series of self-superseding ideals: a limit ever approached, never attained. Thirdly, there are writers who wish (understandably) to incorporate not only ideals but also actualities within their religious vision. Central place may be given to the forces that have worked throughout the evolutionary past to realize life and mind, and which now support them. Such an 'evolutionary humanism' looks back at the pre-human past with wonderment and a scientific concern to understand: it sees man's task as the continuing of this great sweep of development—by new and different ('psycho-social') means. Some may choose to call this a trend towards a 'divinizing' of existence: or call the totality of mind-producing and life-enhancing forces 'divine creativity' or even 'God'. There are many other options, but this selection will give us more than enough to discuss.

We can ask now in more detail: when a humanist presents such a religious reconstruction, by what criteria can it be appraised?

One obvious test to apply is that of internal consistency and coherence. Dewey, in his influential *A Common Faith*, can be faulted on this, since he oscillated between incompatible accounts of 'God'. God should be thought of as "a unification of ideal values", ideals acknowledged "at a given time and place" as authoritative; but also as "connected with all the natural forces and conditions . . . that promote the growth of the ideal" (*op. cit.*, pp. 43, 42, 50). These are by no

36

means the same: nor are they the only accounts Dewey offers.[1]

The phrase 'unification of ideal values' raises a second and different coherence-problem. Although the idea of such a unification stimulates and edifies, it is quite another thing (but surely necessary) to show in some detail that ideals can *admit* of unification. We may speak impressively of an 'imaginary focus' or a 'limit', but we have to show that our set of developing ideals and excellences is at least convergent and not divergent. I cannot persuade my own ideals to show definite convergence; nor am I clear that we are really entitled to speak of a trend towards unity. On the face of it, all goods, all virtues, all forms of beauty are *not* convergent, or 'compossible'. The goods of society and of solitude, active and passive enjoyments, creating and appreciating, the heroic and the unobtrusively decent, the grandly beautiful, the minutely exquisite: these show little tendency to merge in higher syntheses or come to any focus. Our first test, then, insists not only on consistency in definitions but also on a measure of concreteness and detail in the working out of the reconstructive programme. It is not enough that the religious motif should be announced in trumpet-tones, if nothing substantial comes after the fanfare.

A second test is a specifically religious one. Does the 'goal' or 'focus' or empiricist conception of God really meet the main demands of a developed religious consciousness? If we cannot

[1] Compare H. N. Wieman's criticisms of Dewey, in *Intellectual Foundation of Faith*, 1961, Chapter 2.

be animists or polytheists, for instance, that is because we can no longer think of deity as rooted to particular spaces and times, as having the individuality of things-in-the-world. However we conceive it, the divine must be the unconditionally and uniquely great. A humanist or other agnostic cannot, of course, retain all the strands of meaning in a developed notion of deity. So many strands may have to go that he may be far wiser to shy clear of the terms 'God', 'divine', 'holy' altogether. If he does use them, he should at least take care to avoid the grossest anomalies.

For example: if his object of religious concern is the cluster of ideals to which he is now committed, a nasty dilemma appears. As these ideals develop, deepen, change, so the divine must be said to change. And it goes against our religious grain to call that divine which is subject to any change and mutability. The alternative is to deny that the ideals can change—to deliver them from criticism by dogmatic decree. If the first option is religiously offensive, the second is morally reactionary and impossible to the humanist.

So there are advantages in identifying the religious objective not with a set of existent ideals but with, say, an ultimate and perfect transformation of these. We could not be expected to *imagine* this transformation, since to imagine it would be to achieve it. Such a move would certainly restore divine changelessness. Within naturalist assumptions, admittedly, 'ultimate' is a puzzling, maybe confused idea—unless we return to the notion of imaginary focus or of a limit approached but never reached.

Supposing we could cope with the problems about "unification" or weaken the demand for unifying, such a view of the religious objective could be viable, even if many people would find it rather rarefied and bodiless. What it can very well embody, to its great merit, is a combination of dedicated moral seriousness (and an attempt to express as pregnantly and powerfully as possible the content of moral ideals), with a sustained, impassioned criticism of those very ideals as conceived at any one time.[1]

We expect a religious orientation, whether Christian, or humanist, not only to answer questions about aspirations and ideals, but also about the relation of man to his world. Is the universe friendly to man, does it endorse his purposes and values, ignore them or mock them? How ought we to comport ourselves *vis-à-vis* our large-scale environment, its present and its past: what should be our attitudes—acceptance, resignation, rebellion, trust? In the end, the attitudes we adopt must be judged reasonable or absurd according to our total imaginative view of what the world is like. Again, the crucial question is: with such and such a religious outlook, what attitudes am I *entitled* to adopt—confidence, joy, because underneath are the everlasting arms; resentment, despair, exhilaration, indifference, because underneath are no arms at all?

Two extreme positions are possible here, and many intermediate ones between them. (i) Our religious view may be entirely aspirational, in

[1] My few paragraphs of 'constructive conclusions' in fact build upon this sort of view.

that we have no hope or expectation that our ideals will ever be realized, far less permanently or 'eternally'. (ii) If we are theists, we may believe that all value is eternally realized in God, and that his power makes possible a 'conservation of values'. The intermediate positions vary in their degrees of optimism and pessimism, according to their accounts of nature's 'co-operation', 'indifference' or 'hostility'.

Suppose that someone is working out a humanist faith which he wishes to have a buoyant, 'dynamic', bracing tone, and which will see the human task as an energetic continuing of the great evolutionary march. Then he will be strongly tempted to bolster morale by statements like these: 'nature is the cradle of life, mind and value': 'nature is hospitable to value, and co-operates with man in its development.' But such statements need a close scrutiny. They are richly ambiguous. They can refer in very different ways to very different points of our spectrum. It is precisely these kinds of statement that can bluster us into assuming attitudes and feeling emotions that may be far from warranted by what we admit to be the facts.

'Nature is hospitable to mind and value' may mean only this: that certain beings have emerged, on this planet at least, with mental and moral capacities. The present physical conditions on the planet allow these beings to exist and multiply. But the evolutionary processes through which life and mind have developed are themselves entirely mindless and purposeless, and nature's 'hospitality' is of a drastically limited kind. The planet will not support life in an unbounded future;

40

death puts a term to the individual's pursuit of value; and his death may be due to the workings of lowly organisms thriving at the expense of the higher. This precariousness and vulnerability—if we are deeply conscious of it—makes 'hospitality' much too bland and optimistic a word. 'Tolerance' at the most, or 'temporary tolerance' is all we can say.

It could be argued, however, that this is to swing too far in the other direction—towards an unwarranted pessimism. We experience more than a bare, grudging toleration of the conditions of life. These conditions might have been realized, for instance, in a world far less aesthetically exciting than is the real world. And even if aesthetic and religious experiences both are subjective, projected on the screen of nature by our own imaginations, nature 'takes' our projectings, lends itself in the most enthralling, if tantalizing, ways to our seeing of visions and dreaming of dreams. On the theoretical level, the world is not opaque to our understanding; and, on the practical, it offers scope for sustained and concerted action, technological, social and moral. It is not absurd to call it 'a vale of soul-making': statements about nature's co-operation and hospitality are really not so misleading.

And yet: if it is a vale of soul-making, the world can also be a vale of soul-destroying. Suffering may give scope for noble heroism but it also can take the nobility out of a life.[1] If scope is offered for adventure, so also is the possibility of real and undeserved loss—with no restitution

[1] See, for instance, D. M. MacKinnon's remarks in *Objections to Christian Belief*, pp. 23f.

(on a humanist view) in any hereafter. This now makes room for the sublimities of tragedy: but it also admits quite undramatic miseries, the wastes of loneliness, anxiety or depression.

None of these pictures is *false*: they are all partial. They serve simply to remind us that with a slightly different emphasis, a shift in selection of data, of aspect, of metaphor, there goes a corresponding shift in the attitudes that are properly to be taken up towards our large-scale environment. Some of these metaphors are of immense imaginative power. They tug and clamour to be given their heads and to control our complete response to our world. They want us to see life, for instance, as Adventure, Soul's Journey. We *can* see it like that: the attitude is readily evoked—even with the most meagre outfit of beliefs and expectations. But, notoriously, this theme of 'venture' is most exposed to sabotage, it balances often between sublime and ridiculous, it totters on the brink of the fatuous. What makes it so unstable is just the complexity of things—the complexity of which we have been reminding ourselves rather laboriously. This complexity seems to make it impossible to assume any *single* attitude, like rebellion, indifference, or glad acceptance, towards the large-scale environment, for there seems always some factor, some ignored feature of our situation that will make nonsense of it.

The reconstructor is thus in a very different position from the theist. To measure the difference is to measure the difficulty of his task. The appropriateness of attitudes that a theist is entitled to take up to the world is guaranteed by

42

the unchanging purposiveness of its Creator, in whose hand the world is. He does not have to try to read the expression on the face of the universe —smiling, louring or sardonic. *Not* doing that is part of what it means to believe in transcendence.

The Christian doctrine of divine creation, which is also a doctrine of divine sustaining, can readily be made to give an account of evolutionary history in terms of God's purpose. A single trajectory of purpose underlies the whole cosmic process. This gives to an immense diversity of events a kind of unity, a homogeneity in terms of divine action.

An evolutionary humanist wants to replace that view with a non-theistic one, in which the cosmic process was not purposed or controlled or modified by any intelligent being, not at least until man appeared, but in which the vision of a *single sweep of development* towards life and mind still stands out dramatically. The humanist's vision is an imaginative construction, a construction from innumerable heterogeneous events over a vast period of time.

Imaginative constructions have their own peculiar hazards. They can be purely fanciful and superficial, a froth of fragile analogies, distant resemblances taken for identities, the untypical fragment taken to represent the whole. Or, at the other pole, they can be profound, just and comprehensive. It is premature to say that the evolutionary humanist view is the one or the other: for the view is still being articulated. But we can list some further anxieties, and try to ensure that the difficulties are fully seen.

43

The main difficulty, I suspect, is that of faithfully remembering the heterogeneity of the events that make up the evolutionary process, while struggling towards a 'single-sweep' image. With the word 'evolution' the humanist is referring to all the factors of interplay between organism and environment which have modified species, led some to dominance, some to extinction, others to developmental dead-ends. Just how diversified these factors are, the biologist knows far better than the philosopher.

It is hard to keep such diversity before the mind, and in working out an evolutionary humanism, it is most tempting to simplify, even to personify evolution, to make it again, surreptitiously, an agent, the Bringer-about, the Promoter, of ever higher forms of life. It is hard also to remember constantly the mindlessness of the 'trend towards mind'.

One point of discontinuity—of transition at least—which the evolutionary humanist admits is the shift to the 'psycho-social' phase of evolution. Man has become an autonomous moral agent, able to plan out his own pattern of living and increasingly able today to control the economy of his planet. But this distinctively human contribution is still to be thought of as a contribution to 'further evolution'. There is surely an awkwardness here, for the religious-minded evolutionary humanist. In the first place, if he is to achieve his wonder-evoking evolutionary vision, the continuity of the whole process (human phase included) needs to be stressed. Now, in the pre-human phases there was no morality at all, and the humanist's morality cannot be adequately

44

described as a continuation of pre-moral evolutionary mechanisms by conscious means. It is, of
course, in many respects, *opposed* to these, as the
humanist will not deny. His is no tooth-and-claw
morality. But secondly, the more we acknowledge
the differences between morality and any earlier
mechanisms of evolutionary change, the harder
it is to hold the entire process together as a single,
religiously and morally impressive vision. In
moments of deep moral perplexity, it is not to such
a vision that a man could turn with hope of
fresh insight or reassurance.

These remarks are relevant not only to reconstructions that explicitly take 'evolution' as
their key concept. The same sort of problems
appear if 'creativity', for instance, is given that
role. Let the expression 'creativity' or 'divine
creativity' refer to all the natural forces and
conditions that led up to the emergence of a free,
morally responsible, aesthetically productive
humanity. Let it refer also to everything that
fosters this moral and aesthetic life, that pushes it,
by way of restless self-criticism, towards endlessly
improved modes of thought and action. Without
doubt, an impressive vision can be worked out
along these lines.

If we ask how well-grounded and stable such a
view can be, misgivings crowd back upon us.
There is in fact no one thing, or power, or single
continuing process of which 'creativity' is the
name: and many of the processes by which
human creativity has been made possible have
been blind, even destructive processes. As before,
the heterogeneous and often alien character of
the ingredients is screened from us by the

45

impressiveness of the key concept. The risks of self-deception are at their highest if we use the word 'God' for this imaginative construction, as is done, for instance, by H. N. Wieman. "The language about God [refers] to what creates, sustains, saves and transforms toward the greater good" (*Intellectual Foundation of Faith*, p. 50). If we mean by creativity precisely what creates, sustains, saves and transforms in this way, what is improper about equating it with God? It misleads for a familiar reason. Strongly implied in the language of deity is that what creates, sustains, transforms is always the *same* intelligent future-pre-viewing "One"; or at least that there exists somewhere, somehow, a single source, a powerhouse, of creativity. (Compare Wieman *op. cit.*, pp. 22f., 46–57.) Wieman goes as far as to say that God, so interpreted, can actually *love* (*op. cit.*, p. 75). If one wants commonsensically to protest that a God who is not a transcendent individual cannot do any loving, Wieman replies,

> Here . . . is a case of narrow vision. If love means to create, sustain, save from evil and creatively transform . . . , then in that sense God in the form of creativity is the very substance of love. Of course if one means by divine love that God must have that state of consciousness which I experience in myself when I say that I love, then we cannot say that God has any such ambiguous, instable and mixed set of feelings such as I call love in myself. Thank God that God does not love as I do! (*Ibid.*, *loc. cit.*)

Surely here is a case not merely of wide vision

46

but also of a misleadingly wide redefinition of
'love'. If any concept was tailor-made to express
essentially *personal* relationships, one would have
thought it was 'love'. The instability and im-
purity of human love do not derive primarily
from its being a conscious and affective state: to
think of these aspects as eliminated is not to
purify but to nullify our conception of love. The
high-solemn claim that 'God loves' amounts to
no more than this: that those (non-personal)
forces which create, sustain etc. do in fact create,
sustain, etc., and on the other hand those that
don't, don't.[1]

The language of religion, in a humanist context, tends to be embarrassingly over-rich in
metaphysical meanings and suggestions. What
are unities of imagination come to appear, under
its power, unities of fact. What is one possible
attitude to nature (its friendliness or hostility to
value) comes to look the only legitimate view.
The task of a critique is to restore a sense of
complexity, awareness of the multitude of optional
attitudes, the diversity under the apparent unity.

I want now to intensify and to broaden this
general line of criticism. The chief difficulty over
attitudes was the wealth of alternative selections
of data (all of them necessarily partial) on which
the proper, stable, religious attitude was to be
based. But the problem is even more intractable
than that. The *same* selections of data often allow
conflicting interpretations.

Think, for instance, of attitudes to the human

[1] In fairness, these criticisms touch only a small part of Wieman's
position, with much of which I am in thorough agreement.

body and its evolutionary development. There is room for wonderment at its prodigies of adaptation, the cunning of the eye's mechanism, the extraordinary intricacies of the brain: but there is room also for anxiety, even dread, that we are utterly dependent upon these vulnerable organs for our well-being, our very existence; that we are separated from nothingness by the thickness (or thinness) of an artery-wall.

How, again, shall we view our domination of the planet, our uniqueness (there at least) as a thinking, choosing, self-determining being?—if we like, we can view it with solemn exhilaration; but again, if we like, with a sense of bleak loneliness, as an affirmer of values in a realm where value is otherwise unknown.

The same phenomena which figure in our vision of the glorious evolutionary sweep towards mind can be viewed with repugnance—as involving centuries of ceaseless animal suffering, of killing and being killed.[1]

What we look for here but fail to find are ways of resolving the ambiguities, of guiding and controlling our interpretation. The traditional faiths do provide such controls—at least for the most important choices of attitude. Both grandeur and misery may characterize man on a Christian view: yet the doctrines of creation and redemption steer the believer from the extremes of Promethean pride or a total vilifying of man. It is only with the help of such doctrinal controls that stable, wholehearted and clear-cut religious atti-

[1] There is a problem of evil outside theism, contrary to what is usually argued. Only, it is a problem of the conflict of attitudes, not of doctrines.

48

tudes are maintained. In Christianity the chief of these are attitudes *to God* and his purposes, and can therefore be (like these purposes) unfluctuating. This stability and wholeheartedness are religiously important. Their absence is debilitating. To revere—but only to a point; to marvel—but only to such and such an extent; to wonder—from this viewpoint, but to be bored or horrified from the other: these ambiguities and qualifications seem inevitable in any humanist religious outlook, unless it works wholly on the level of ideals and aspirations.

If this be so, it injects a measure of irony into humanist claims to be the 'emancipators' of religion. "For the first time," wrote Dewey, "the religious aspect of experience will be free to develop freely on its own account" (*A Common Faith*, pp. 2, 44). Religion is to be delivered from such "encumbrances" as the supernatural and the dubiously historical: but freed also, we have to add, from the controls that gave firm direction and stability to its attitudes and evaluations.

III

This is a book of Objections, and I have therefore been dutifully, if rather lugubriously, objecting, raising difficulties, chastening complacency. Since, however, my attitude to religious 'reconstructing', though cautious, is actually far from hostile, I am tempted to change mood before ending, and to hazard a more hopeful coda. Its suggestions will be of the most tentative, interim kind.[1]

[1] There is some indebtedness here to writings of Walter Kaufmann, J. N. Findlay and others.

First, I want to say that this work of criticism on which we have been engaged has itself a religious aspect. It is continuous with the religious task of overthrowing idols, of superseding inadequate notions of deity, with the quest for the 'God behind god'. What survives of it here is the readiness to probe, to discredit if need be, the current objects of religious and moral veneration, to accept disillusionment in the name of honesty, and even to make that disillusionment as thorough as it can be made.

Often enough, religion has built up men's hopes and expectations in most massive but ill-justified ways: its glories and colours have been the shimmerings of a too-far-stretched film of analogies and metaphors. Yet religion has not only been this; it has also been the quest for fuller understanding of whatever objects are held to be glorious and great, and the scrutiny of their credentials. This it should continue to be. Perhaps the credentials of no single existent thing can satisfy our demands for an adequate object of religious worship. If so, our faith has to be primarily aspirational, a constant attempt to express, embody and again transcend the best moral and aesthetic conceptions that can be attained. Even if we have no God behind god, we have form-of-life behind form-of-life, vision behind vision. I think, however, that we are not limited to a *purely* aspirational faith, fundamental though that will be.

There are certain types of religious experience, senses as of the 'holy', some forms also of mystical experience that, for some people at least, can continue to occur even in agnosticism.

They seem in this sense to be 'autonomous', not belief-dependent, experiences. Even if they are not seen as yielding new knowledge of the world, insights into 'ultimate truth', they can still make a profound mark on a person's moral outlook. They can do so, not by imparting specific new information or specific rules of conduct but by nourishing a sense of wondering openness to new ways, new possibilities of life. They implant a disturbing restlessness, a *nisus* towards the transformation of ideals, an intensified dissatisfaction with the mean, drab or trivial. I say that these experiences *can* do this, not that all necessarily do. It is possible merely to play with mystical or quasi-mystical experiences, as aesthetic luxuries or exotic thrills—especially if they are induced by artificial means. Just as—drugs apart—a discipline of perception and response is necessary for evoking such experiences, so a further, related discipline is needed through which to bind them to the moral life. The absence of theistic belief does not mean that these links are weak and artificial. Mystical experience, in many if not all of its forms, is experience of reconciliation, the breaking down of barriers of individuality. It can be brought into intimate relation with movements of thought and feeling in morality, such as sympathetic identification with others, escape from egocentricity to the stance of charity. Nature-mystical experiences, even in quite lowly and undeveloped forms, can foster and reinforce attitudes of contemplative gentleness and restraint in our dealings with nature, and can act as a powerful corrective to the dominant attitudes of technological man. In the light of them, we

51

can no longer see the world simply as our quarry, our rubbish tip, ours to consume or ravish or to take as spoil.

What attitude, finally, can a religiously-minded agnostic take up to the literature of the traditional faiths? It is in these, in Upanishads, Pali Canon, Old and New Testaments . . . that we can watch the religious vocabulary actually being forged, can watch the sifting and winnowing of idolatrous from worthy notions of the divine. Without a lively awareness of the meanings of terms like 'holy', 'sinful', 'Nirvana', in the full complexity of their original contexts and in subsequent development, we cannot know what we are doing in setting such words to new tasks; we cannot know what work we are continuing.

The more seriously these writings are studied, however, the more unthinkable it becomes to see them as antique shops from which to pick up a few useful and adaptable pieces of religious furniture. This could be one more act of irreverent despoliation. For the great religions have a unity that makes it difficult for individual ideas extracted from them to lead an independent life.

On the other hand, a sympathetic reading of the great theistic or mystical works can awaken certain sorts of religious response (of which we have just spoken) that do seem able to survive the death of their parent body of belief: and perhaps to thrive. Theology itself admits it can speak of these only stammeringly and in paradoxes. Words fail: and this very failure may show that there is nothing here tailor-made to a single system of ideas. But to awaken those responses in the first place, and even stammeringly allude to them, a near-indispensable means is the study of those same scriptures, and the literature of poetry and meditation that derives from them.

This is to commend an approach to the scriptures that strenuously combines (yet again) the devotional and the critical. There must be imaginative effort to see the world through the various lenses or filters of the religions, and an equally serious scrutiny of what any of these views really presuppose, how far they involve now-discredited beliefs, one-sided selections of data, the ignoring of deep ambiguities. There must be vigorous attempts to sift out what really is autonomous from what only seems to be so.

Towards what goal would such a view be working? Certainly not towards an eclectic 'harmony' of the great religions, or a new religious ideology for the Western World. And probably not towards any religious resting-place, any stable 'position'. What we should be doing above all is keeping alive the religious imagination and simultaneously confronting its products with a searching, uninhibited rational critique: setting partial vision against vision, as it were chord against chord in an unresting, taut progression.

If this is no recipe for relaxed living, it at least avoids two dangers to which humanists and other naturalists are exposed and which can sap moral and intellectual integrity. The one reduces the essence of all religion to a common vague and harmless numinosity—with which even the unbeliever, if he feels inclined, can enhance or decorate his own outlook. Against this, serious comparative studies make it plain that there is *no* essence of religion, and that mysteries (as I put it earlier) are not interchangeable.

The other danger is of identifying a religion with its doctrinal formulae, and with the arguments of its apologists. A paradox here, an ill-grounded historical claim there—and we have the right to consider it overthrown. Against that, this essay has insisted on the *complexity* of religious claims and attitudes. Given flaws of logic or evidence, much needs to be abandoned—more than some humanists suspect. There may survive, however, moral concepts of a richness that shows up the meagreness of the humanist's own. And there may survive ways of seeing humanity, transfigurations of the supposedly familiar world, which—even when we are quite unable to assimilate or domesticate them—can haunt and trouble and goad the imagination.

Is

Rationalism

Sterile ?

KATHLEEN NOTT

SOMEBODY once said that "There is something ridiculous about a married philosopher", and this may well have been the opinion of Xantippe too. Indeed those engaged in the life of the mind have never seemed to think excessively highly of the institution of marriage, although, as far as I can make out, contemporary English philosophers in much higher proportion than has ever been known, are benedicts. This may not mean much more than that universities are no longer semi-monastic institutions. Or it may mean too that in our day philosophy has become less a vocation and more a profession. Nevertheless, for whatever cause, it may be granted that the proportion of celibates among intellectuals of all kinds was

55

until lately very high, not least among philosophers, the most abstract thinkers: Kant, Nietzsche, Peirce, Bradley—there are plenty more. This does not mean, as every schoolboy knows, that they were 'sterile'. *How many children had Kant?* is a realistic speculation, even if we cannot find the answer. And to shun domestic joys and cares does not entail—as the matter was put to me—"inhibition, impoverishment in sensibility and vitality". A great many people have these drawbacks without benefit or fault of excessive intellection.

There is, however, a case for believing that the cerebral type is at least as bad as everyone else in forming satisfactory personal and social relations; and that, in this direction, philosophers are not markedly 'philosophical' nor rationalists 'rational'. Moreover, I should not deny that there is a necessary, and a valuable, distinction to be drawn between the logical or analytical kind of intelligence, and the kind which employs itself in imagination and feeling; nor that, in some cases, this may amount to a real opposition, even a mutual exclusion.

Dislike and fear of the cerebral may be prejudiced, whether it is vulgar and uninformed or, as with D. H. Lawrence, mystical and solar-plexal, but it asks for serious consideration because, if for no other reason, it reflects a dispute which throughout European history has had wide and potent consequences—and also because, at some levels, it may be a natural and healthy reaction towards what is felt to be a disastrous split in the European mind.

This "dissociation in sensibility", which T. S.

Eliot described, as it affected poetry after the seventeenth century, was real: how far it can be ascribed to the development of scientific naturalism is, I think, more doubtful.

Perhaps we can put the question in this form: Is there an inevitable clash between thinking and feeling?

It might be readily agreed that we should try to see the Rationalist in his philosophical history; and also that the empirical anti-metaphysical strain has become dominant in the last three centuries of thought. But I shall suggest in the pages that follow, that the rationalist is also a certain kind of mind and personality; that we have to consider him too in his subjective history; and that this approach is applicable as well to the philosophers who have influenced him, and will be indeed more illuminating in the case of these 'objective' and professionally abstract thinkers.

Philosophers are inevitably cerebral, and nowadays often agnostic. Nevertheless, not only philosophers, but scientists and mathematicians in our time have often a real and penetrating concern with the arts. The common association of music and mathematics is well known. Dr Bronowski for one has made notable efforts to bring poetry and science together, and he has also shown (in *Science and Human Values*) a marked awareness that moral and aesthetic values are not ultimately to be separated.

Some of those too who earlier in this century, in the controversy about meaning and value, adopted a rigidly scientific standard for 'meaning', have come more and more to regard poetry as the language of unified apperception, the language

57

indeed of our common and real awareness: Professor I. A. Richards is a striking example. His own more recent publications have been volumes of poetry. And there are scientists in the strict sense who write and publish poetry as well as taking a critical interest in it.

This practical concern with poetry and the arts might with some intellectuals express the sense of a personal therapeutic need—like the sick cat which goes instinctively for the grass. But it may well be nothing more than an intelligent and healthy recognition that every human mind must learn to balance itself. Where there is a great variety of desires, interests and propensities a deliberate effort may be needed if these are to be in harmony instead of conflict.

It remains probable that in all human beings the powers of selection, concentration, absorption and relation have necessary and reciprocal limitations and no doubt we are highly unlikely to meet an absolutely equal development of logic and analysis, on the one hand, and imagination and intuition, on the other, in one mind and personality.

Moreover if we look at what we know of the personal history of those who have preferred to think in general and abstract terms we shall unquestionably find a great deal of the obsessional anxiety which we nowadays describe as neurotic. Descartes, Kant, Nietzsche and Schopenhauer, to mention only a few, would certainly not have qualified as A1 at Freud's. Wittgenstein was severely depressive, and the late J. L. Austin, who so obsessively fascinated many of his fellow Oxford philosophers might well, to judge by the narrow calibre of his murderously sharpened philosophic instrument, have been himself obsessional. The analytical and generalizing intellect, particularly in its mathematical and logical specialization, seems too narrow for a maturing humanity, and I would even suggest that it may be allied with an actual dislike of the concrete particulars of ordinary spontaneous living.

Professor Wisdom indeed once made a deliberate (and entertaining) comparison between philosophic and obsessive 'doubt'. For instance, the professional philosopher may produce the interrogative sentence "Did I turn off the gas?" in order to illustrate the nature of doubt and certainty. The obsessional neurotic may ask the same question. What precisely is the distinction? We may say at once that the philosopher knows what he is doing; but in a certain sense so often does the neurotic. However, the philosopher also knows that his sentence is merely the pattern of a possible experience, not the reflection of a real one; whereas with the neurotic this is not necessarily the case. (Moreover the neurotic will very likely go back to find out, without ever reaching final conviction.) And lastly, the philosopher can leave off, as the neurotic, anyway after a time, cannot.

I myself, however, think that the contrast between the two subjectivities, the philosophic and the neurotic, is not quite so sharp as these common-sense distinctions might suggest. Professor Wisdom's joke was partly in earnest.

Philosophers, any more than the rest of humanity, do not spring fully armed out of their own heads; and it seems highly unlikely that their

59

interests and adult careers were not partly chosen, at an early age, by their biological and psychological history. Cerebration, one may say, always tries to control experience, rather than to submit to it. Leaving aside the value of the fruits, what the philosopher's disposition shares with the neurotic's (whatever its intellectual level) is the liking for generalizations and the temptation to immure and fortify himself in them. (I leave aside too the comparative validity of the generalizations. We will assume of course that a philosopher's training and ethos have alike conditioned him against premature and uncritical generalization; the point of comparison lies in the subjective aim.)

In the neurotic, the subjective aim is uncritical; but it is instinctually and emotionally similar. To me personally, and especially for the purpose of my present discussion, the most interesting aspect of neurotic mental conditions is just this obsessional obligation to build generalizing castles in the air, and to refuse to emerge from them. At a critical age of his development, the person who is to reveal himself as neurotic may feel himself naked in the face of the world of the Other, a new world which he fears too much to understand. What is more likely than that he will try to master it, to control it, with generalizations which appear to be knowledge, but which as description are false or totally inadequate, and must remain so because he cannot afford to put them to the test?

The need for a kind of emotional security which is humanly unobtainable is obvious in the neurotic, and in his case it is, I suggest, the decisive factor—the quest for certainty, a need for final answers on which he may rest and which will also relieve him from the ordinary human obligation to make moment-to-moment personal decisions for which he must take responsibility. This need for certainty or finality might partly account for the suicidal wishes of many neurotics. Death is inevitable—so let us have done with it.

What, except as a metaphoric parallel, has all this in common with the processes of philosophers or other professional and abstract thinkers? It has often been remarked by contemporary philosophers who have any wryness or levity, or perhaps any modest self-observation, that the process of philosophizing is a mighty odd one. Apart from Wisdom, F. E. Sparshott, for instance (*An Enquiry Into Goodness*), strongly suggests that you do it in order to stop it. To Wittgenstein it was a therapy to remove an uncomfortable sense of puzzlement. And others, L. L. Whyte, for one example, have also believed that thinking is undertaken to come to the end of thinking. There is at least this much agreement here—that thinking is a painful effort, even for those who are most in training, and that you would not do it if you could help it. It is a compulsion which conflicts with your passive and vegetative side. To most people, indeed, it is unnatural and repugnant, and at their own level, whatever that may be, they get along quite well without trying. I am not attributing superiority to the select and odd band of people who have a bent for abstract ratiocination when I say that in this sense the majority does not think at all. For in another sense, we all think—human beings and animals

61

alike—when we have to solve an encountered practical problem.

Practical thinking, may involve people in further effort—as politicians, artists, doctors, housewives, lovers or soldiers—but it is a much more pleasing pain than that of the philosopher, because its fruits are soon seen to be ripening, or its errors become visible and bring relief, and because it has intervals in which you can go to bed or on holiday. With philosophizing there is no guarantee that this will be the case. A philosopher's work is much more like Alice's flamingo —when you tuck in its head its feet stick out. This can be dispiriting and frustrating to philosophers who let themselves be honestly aware of their human and emotional needs. Among great philosophers, Hume, who hung his nose as far as any over the nihilistic abyss, withdrew it sharply when he saw the psychological risks involved and advised dilution of metaphysics by playing backgammon and making merry with friends. The conclusion of Hume's philosophizing was indeed a radical scepticism which left no convincing logical grounds for believing that anything natural, let alone supernatural, was there at all, and he saved his 'reason' or, we might say, his 'philosophical personality'—for he had, or he acquired, the temperamental serenity and wisdom which is popularly, if wrongly, associated with the philosopher—by refusing to take the implications of his philosophy to heart. Hume's cheerfulness, good nature, generosity and integrity make it easy for us to accept what in others we should uncomfortably suspect to be cynicism. But it seems likely that, as well as fathering the epistemological problems which have kept present-day philosophers busy, his detachment from practical applications or consequences has also influenced them—undesirably, as some think.

If there is indeed some kind of hereditary succession from Hume, our contemporary philosophers' detachment from the problems which interest and often involve other men, is still of a different quality from his, and serves a different purpose and motivation. Up to Hume's day at least it was still possible for philosophers to be amateurs and either to dabble in or to try to relate a number of interests. Hume was for instance a historian. His work on ethics is perhaps more interesting than is always allowed today. This may have been because Hume's vital inconsistency was allowed its proper play. One might even say that his ethical writings come more from the man of the world, from the side of "backgammon and friends" than from the sceptical philosopher. Certainly he did not regard rationality as a motive force: "Reason is and ought only to be the slave of the passions".

It is possible—and this is a point of view I shall try to develop—that the most fruitful kind of thinking, which unites theory and practice, comes out of a passive attitude towards experience. (To be passive does not exclude being expectant, looking in particular directions.) The natural, practical or amateur thinker thinks largely to make up his own mind in order to know what to do next. He is trying to see for himself what is there, how it is related and what, if anything, can or ought to be done about it. In this sense his 'logic', the particular structure of his thinking, is formed by his circumstances. His concern—unlike that of many contemporary philosophers—is not with final or incorrigible statements, but with results that work. (And if they do work it is no good saying that they don't.)

Moreover it may be doubted whether a course in modern logic or the study of modern philosophy will help this kind of thinker (including the working scientist) to think any more productively or for that matter more clearly. Present-day philosophers are talking about something else, usually language, and their kind of logic may not be directly applicable to other fields. The reason why they do not write much about ethics, aesthetics, history, politics, psychology, even biology, may even be because they are not sufficiently open-minded towards these other kinds of living and practical experience and the new conceptual insights, the different kinds of 'logic' which these force upon their committed students. We must add that certain 'rationalists', especially of the older school, resemble these philosophers in being insufficiently open-minded towards experience, in trying to impose their own patterns of argument, and in rejecting as absurd or nonsensical what will not fit in with it. In other words, this kind of rationalist is not *sufficiently* agnostic. It is not the patient waiting on evidence which makes for sterility in any kind of thinking, but rather dogmatism, concealed or overt. (This is always waiting round the corner for all of us.)

The situation in philosophy is changing, I believe, and it is no longer intellectually disreputable to produce works on ethics and

64

aesthetics, or even to specialize in these subjects. But in this country I should say we have a long way to go before philosophers, like their continental contemporaries, particularly some existentialists, feel bound to take poetic and imaginative thinking seriously.

That they do not means that the "dissociation in sensibility" is still with us. The explanation I suggest is that through historical conditioning, the quest for certainty, for final demonstration or proof has, whether deliberately or not, become the standard of philosophical investigation. (That this finality is humanly unobtainable does not alter the situation.) Other factors intensify the drive, for instance the stress, both popular and philosophical, which is laid on the *success* of scientific precision and demonstration—although this is not of necessity the most important aspect of scientific thinking.

There is something, too, to be attributed to professionalism. Most philosophers nowadays have jobs in universities. The obligation to produce more generations of philosophers (and disciples) combined with the close domestic life with colleagues may sharpen the wits but it also sharpens the axes. Proof, making one's point, become main objectives: hence competition and avoidance of issues where success is less obvious and longer in maturation.

If it is thus true that our philosophers have been historically infected by the passion for a final objectivism, it is no wonder that their energies have become wholly diverted towards logic and epistemology, towards the structure of thinking and the nature or possibility of knowledge, rather

65

than towards ethics and aesthetics which inevitably have one foot in the flux of existence and from which no one really expects final conclusions.

The philosophers' preoccupation with language can also be seen in the same light, as motivated by the ideal of a perfect language of incorrigible statements in which, and only in which, you could say exactly what you mean, and only what you mean. A strong presumption arose in our time that ordinary language is not wholly suitable for even the social sciences—if you can't reduce what you want to say to mathematical formulation it may be neither clear nor meaningful. (There have even been some attempts in this direction in literary criticism.) And contemporary philosophy has continued to be haunted beyond utility by Wittgenstein's idea of language as a map or picture of the world—*photograph*, we might rather say, because the scale implied is inconceivably larger than any map or picture. It looks as if the earlier Wittgenstein had a hankering to turn the world into words.

Language, however, is not a photographic record and it does not serve the ideal of complete correspondence with the world of experience. But if we take it in its widest sense of communication (as linguistic philosophers do not necessarily do) it is perhaps the most important instrument of human exchange and vision and of orientation and change in our environment. It does not have to be a tight fit: play, as with a loose sleeve, is necessary for its proper functioning.

It seems to be probable that the interest in 'common usage' or 'ordinary language' which developed partly as a reaction to the earlier work of Wittgenstein has not really outmoded the chimerical ideal of building a finally precise and perfectly correct language—for it is the standard of language, not the revealing idiosyncrasies, in which philosophers are interested. If you could have a perfectly correct, perfectly correspondent language, it is doubtful whether you could say anything in it that really mattered to anybody. For if it is better to say nothing than to say what might be nonsense or might be given a multiple interpretation, tautology (the perfectly certain, perfectly empty pronouncement that *A is A*) seems the only safe course.

The language of ordinary men and women is more like that of poets, or even lovers, than that of philosophers, even of philosophers who have devoted themselves to 'ordinary usage'. Philosophers aim at finding the incorrigible propositions, the irreducible bricks of discourse. Ordinary language is not only persistently evaluative, it licks its way round meaning as subtly as flame. It is always saying too, *What I like or dislike, what interests or bores me.* By saying what I see through the window of the self, it is always building a bridge between an inner and an outer, assumed, world. And to *say* is a transitive verb, like to *know*. To say is always to say something. It is also to assume that there is something there to say something about; that one lives in, and is a living part of, a real and living world, which asserts itself and promises *some* significance prior to human understanding or analysis. As Hume implied, we can't prove the world and its causal connections. We work by animal faith.

It is this animal faith that not only extreme rationalists, but modern western intellectuals, including many philosophers, are short of. It has recently been remarked that although a number of Oxford philosophers are actually practising Christians, as well as of many other shades of religious belief, they are all of them in the sense I am describing *agnostics*. The extreme rationalist, of course, almost by definition, won't believe anything unless he *sees reason*.

Why after all should he? Because, I suppose, we have to live and it is by this animal faith that we do live. To be too analytical, to demand explanations, reasons and logical or moral justifications can, we know, destroy human trust and therefore human relations. And if such destruction is not sterile, I do not know what is. But the psychological attitude is probably prior to the intellectual. Safeguarding, the longing for final reassurance characterizes all of us, rationalists and religious alike, and the prestige of objective proof is only an intellectual parallel.

It seems to me that the 'theologians' on either side of the rationalist-supernaturalist controversy have become mere case-makers, primarily out for proofs. (Natural enough, no doubt, but meanwhile the riches of feeling, religious or human, have been flung out with the bath-water.) It looks as if some kinds of argument, whatever they appear to be about, can indeed be largely sterile because they are not really aimed at finding a synthesis, a solution, at making peace. They belong to a side, they are covert polemic, and they aim at victory. With warfare of all kinds, truth is indeed the first victim.

There are good psychological and good historical reasons why we all want to be *right*, why we find it difficult to suspend judgement and so to be *truly* 'agnostic', and why we feel that we cannot live from day to day without some sort of systematic creed. The habit of demanding objective certainties (in the face of the observed fact that we never get them) is so engrained in the world of the West at least, that a more flexible, perhaps a more fatalistic conduct seems absurd.

Historically this European attitude has remote and tangled roots. But we can hardly overestimate the historical effect of Cartesianism. Popularly, we think of Descartes as the great Doubter. He claimed that he would maintain complete scepticism towards any belief or statement that he could not clearly and unmistakably see to be the case. Whatever benefits this famous 'method' bestowed on mathematics and physics (and of this I am not really competent to speak), it seems obvious that Descartes diverted our philosophical, psychological and imaginative thinking towards dead ends.

For 'Descartes the Doubter' was quite as much the great and anxious seeker after certainty. (Some psychological thought holds that 'safeguarding' is the prescription for anxiety—so it seems did Jesus Christ.) Descartes's vision of a perfect rational certainty was, as we know, an actual dream. It was also a conversion-phenomenon, which made him a changed man with a mission. Conversions usually imply a rejection of other and earlier ways of experiencing, and this seems to have been the case with Descartes. Aiming at perfectly rational intellectual clarity he achieved a split in his own mind, driving the complexity of human life, thought, feeling, and sensuous awareness below the surface. As L. L. Whyte says—"This dream of rationalism betrayed human nature but it shaped the temperament of rationalists from Descartes to Freud." (And after, one must add.) For as has been already said, the only perfectly 'rational' certainty which can be tested and demonstrated at every point and line of its chart, is a tautologous one. The world as it is lived is an uncertain flux.

If we followed Descartes's doubting to its logical conclusion (as he did not do himself) we might easily lose our 'animal faith'. And to identify certainty with the formally abstract and rational is necessarily to demote feeling and sense. The 'split' or dissociation in our characteristically European awareness indeed seems to illustrate this loss of animal or empirical faith. But most of those who have written on this dissociation in sensibility have been critics or literary men—Eliot, Basil Willey, Cleanth Brooks, among others—and many of them, particularly the first two I have mentioned, have had an anti-rationalistic axe to grind, and hold that the split took place *because* we lost a supernaturalist faith.

I believe this aspect, if it can fairly be adduced at all, is secondary. What we lost faith in was instinct and intuition, our sensuous awareness, and our imaginative thinking. The 'Age of Reason', and of dull imagery and abstract generalization in poetry or verse, was due to the philosophers rather than to either the scientists or the agnostics. The philosophers too were

sometimes religiously orthodox. Descartes himself
is an example; for one of the two things of which
he found himself most certain was the existence
of God, which he thought he had demonstrated
by unmistakably clear and rational argument—
an argument, the ontological, which has never
been regarded as satisfactory even by theologians
and was demolished by Kant if by no one else.

It looks as if you cannot rationally demonstrate
the existence of anything; but Anglo-American
philosophers on the whole have not yet truly
resigned themselves to this realization, with which
their continental coevals seem much more at
home. To hold to an extreme standard of rational
demonstration means that not only existence but
many of the activities in which as a species we
cannot help engaging, have to be demoted below
the intellectual salt. Not only poetry (as from the
seventeenth century): by this standard the procedures of science itself can be regarded as
'irrational'. (The logician's worry about a
Principle of Induction—that there is no purely
logical warrant for believing that because something, the sun rising or men dying, for example,
has always happened without exception, it will
ever happen again—has been dealt with in
various ways: by the scientist chiefly by taking no
notice.)

I have deliberately brought in the word
'irrational' at this point and I have put it in
inverted commas, because although I am using
it as in common usage, I believe that common
usage is here at least misleading. All along we
may not have been quite definite about who—or
what—is rationalist; but one thing will be

immediately clear, that on what we actually mean by a rationalist or rationalism, our definition of the irrational must depend. The rationalist-irrationalist nomenclature strikes me as in itself a splendid example of the split in our awareness, of the great *Either-Or* which divides both philosophical and psychological thinking: verifiable meaning *or* nonsense; sensation *or* thought; logic *or* the emotive; poetry *or* science.

There might even be a suggestion of this vicious dichotomy, this assumptive *Either-Or*, if not in the opposition out of which this book and its original counterpart have arisen, at any rate in the way it has been classified. And for this both sides can be held responsible. The two books are respectively named *Objections to Christian Belief* and *Objections to Humanism*. These titles suggest at least to me that a Christian believer cannot be a humanist (which is an assumptive definition, and historically absurd); and, on the other hand, that a humanist is necessarily a rationalist in the nineteenth-century dyed-in-the-wool sense of being almost wholly preoccupied with the question of the existence of God, and with rebutting any supernatural sanction for morality.

This kind of rationalism, I would agree, *is* sterile. But then I would deny that it can be identified with humanism. Humanism to me does not mean something abstract. Rather it means a deep and intimate concern with the full flowering of human potentiality and personality which can only be the experience of real individuals. Of these there are not likely to be too many in any generation. Human development, maturation, becoming human, depend on imaginative insights and vision—artistic, scientific, philosophical, personal and relational—which are bound to be exceptional, as far as we can see at present. They are also mainly achieved by sleep-walkers, people who wake up only after they have done something, and who are therefore not able to exercise any final and detailed control in advance, or even to be clearly aware of their processes until these have become, as it were, alienated from themselves.

The old-style rationalist usually does not like this inevitable aspect of the imaginative processes. His attitude is often an emotional dogmatism. He is, or anyway was, a person who thinks that truth is always objective and he does not understand that the word could legitimately be used to describe subjective honesty, the mere will to find out and to comprehend. He often believes that facts are hard, but also brittle, and have therefore to be defended against wicked liars, who have sometimes been poets or mystics. And being defensive, he is also sometimes angry because he feels that Great Deceptions, from time immemorial, have been practised on the race and on himself. Often with reason, he thinks too that God and Love, divine and human, are to be included among these deceiving conceptions, and that they still have too many false prophets. It is worth noting too that this kind of rationalist often suffers from emotional puritanism. He is not only the doughty champion of Black against White: he suspects any attempt to ungird one's loins, and enjoy the more sensuous and passive experiences. In short he may be afflicted with imaginative poverty.

Let us not, however, indulge in *Either-Or*, and fly to the other extreme, by trying to force an association between imaginative significance, on the one hand, and supernaturalism or orthodox religious belief on the other. Belief in God and another world has no doubt provided a deep spring for certain intense imaginations. But often the kind of conceptions which orthodoxy has made available and to which it has given its authoritative warrant, have merely provided a useful imaginative framework. Graham Greene is I think a case in point. I suspect the Jesuit case-book behind his often tortuous psychological investigations. (I don't deny that they are often artistically convincing too.) Centuries earlier Dante made the imaginative most of Catholic cosmology and psychology. The orthodox view is that the *Paradiso*, which expounds doctrinal blessedness, is better poetry than the *Inferno*, where Dante is following his human and psychological nose through the interstices of doctrine. I do not agree. I do not think that orthodoxy created the imaginative power; it gave Dante a stage and a framework. No less an authority than T. S. Eliot has drawn attention to the badness of most religious verse.

One essential reason why good verse, religious or not, is good, is that it has established a successful relation between the universal and the particular: it has established order in change. Conversely bad verse is bad very often because it has lost its footing in the immediate flux: it has become abstract, rigidly conventional, dogmatic, in the sense that it can be justified only by a theory.

74

This can be applied without much change to all forms of thinking and reasoning. The rationalist is respectable (and reasonable) in so far as he is in permanent but flexible relation to evidence. This means that he is always learning, always open to experience. It does not mean that he will lightly desert a fruitful and convincing path; only that he must have a sense of the immediate, and of significant change. The appeal to the empirical is more important than any abstract construction of argument.

What we have to remember is that the sense of the word rationalist as it is implicit in these essays, the sense which ties it to the empirical and in particular to the anti-supernatural, is comparatively modern. In the historical meaning, rationalism implied the claim that 'pure reason' without empirical appeal could arrive at substantial knowledge of the world. And Descartes, Leibnitz and Spinoza have all been described as Rationalists. In some medieval Catholic philosophers, 'pure reason' is distinguished from natural reason (which presumably depends on observation and evidence).

How you define 'irrational' depends on how you define 'reason'. If (like these earlier 'rationalists') you think there is a *pure reason*, you may be tempted to dismiss that disorderly jumble of facts and events, subjective or external, which we loosely describe as 'Nature', as 'irrational'.

An extreme and entertaining example of this curious opposition was provided by Professor C. S. Lewis in his book *Miracles*. Nature, it seems, while not intelligent, is intelligible, but only because she is "colonized by Reason". Left to

75

herself, Nature can only "kill Rational Thoughts". I have never really understood what this means but I observe that it ignores the fact that 'Nature' is certainly an important part of what we have to think Rational Thoughts about, and that without her stimulation we should hardly think at all.

I adduce this merely as an illustration of the split in thinking about the human mind, in one of its most influential and instructive forms. The real controversy then is not between old-style rationalist, and anti-rationalist, particularly of the religious kind, but between two totally incompatible definitions of reason, both of which are abstractions and both of which, although perhaps in differing degree, stigmatize as 'irrational' what is left over after a somewhat selective abstracting process.

The idealists and the 'theologians', of various kinds, may be the worse offenders, but the agnostic type of rationalist is certainly not immune from this inclination to maintain an artificial split between abstract human rationality and the fields of given or spontaneous experience, which should be its subject matter.

Thus the old-style rationalist may well be a rationalizer (not less than the rest of us). He has to 'see reason', and he often finds difficulty in accepting the irreducibility of certain experiences which may be highly and characteristically human. I have dwelt on aesthetic experience. But 'aesthetic' here could be used to cover sensation and perception in themselves. Sartre's *La Nausée* is an odd and instructive example. His character Roquentin finds that ordinary living perceptions have become faintly disgusting because they cannot be satisfactorily rationalized, reduced to the rational. (We should look very carefully at the Existentialist category of the 'Absurd'. Strictly this may be meant as the non-logical, or non-intellectual, but undoubtedly it carries too a strong flavour of the ridiculous, silly or nonsensical, of what therefore ought to be repudiated.)

In summary, one may say that 'reason' or 'rationality' have historically been claimed by two absolute rivals and that both have hypostatized the concept. At present we are most likely to advance (including in knowledge of what we are talking about) if we give up these terms and talk instead about reasoning or being reasonable. This is to hold a particular relation to reality, to be trying to discover what it is in any circumstances, and to be preparing oneself to be conditioned by it. It may not be easy, it may not always be possible. For we are still prone to delude ourselves about our rational status. (For example, until very recently *men* have thought that they were rational whereas *women* were not.) To force our attention to the fact that rationality has to be earned, that growth is the reward for the victory of reality over fantasy, might turn out to be Freud's most valuable contribution.

Thinking or reasoning is learning to see what is the case. This implies learning to see for oneself, and to back and take responsibility for one's conclusions. That does not mean that one has to be 'right'. I believe that there is a pattern of valid thinking or rational process which is common at all levels to human individuals who are minding their own business, whatever it may be at the given

77

moment. We cannot and we should not try to find a paradigm of thinking or verbalization which is abstractly or absolutely correct. We are thinking correctly if we are thinking for a real purpose in a real 'field'. ('Real' here implies that we have enough receptive humility to correct and adapt our egoistic and whimsical purposes in the particular field of experience.) This appeals to me as rationality, and in so far, but only in so far, as rationalism is thus rational, it cannot be sterile. For this is the method and the only method of effecting a creative adaptation or a fruitful change in our environment. I do not think that humanists have to be rationalists in the old sense. I am not at all sure that all of those who use the title are altogether 'reasonable' in the sense I have tried to define.

Is

Humanism

Utopian?

KINGSLEY MARTIN

I

ONE of the most common criticisms of humanism
is that it is foolishly optimistic, youthfully facile,
a surface philosophy that pretends that a bad
world can be transformed overnight into the best
of all possible worlds. Denying original sin, say
the critics, humanists pretend that man is born
reasonable; it follows that given a good environment he will behave well and that any institution
may be safely swept away once it is shown not to
serve men's greatest happiness. This is to ignore
original sin and the fact of unconscious motivation; it assumes against the evidence that scientific
advance is producing a happier and better world.
In short, humanists are criticized for irrationally

79

believing that irrationality can be cured by an appeal to reason and that men's minds are shaped, not by their inherited stock and disposition, but purely by their circumstances. Thus humanists are said to despise emotional propaganda and religious faith and absurdly to suppose that facts, scientific thinking and common sense will lead to Utopia.

Historically speaking many humanists have been open to these charges. From the eighteenth century, when humanism, the religion of man's progress, was shaped, these basic conceptions have dominated liberal minds. One of humanism's earliest apostles, to take an extreme instance, was the Abbé de St Pierre, who worked out 'projects' for everyone's improvement. We all know that he produced a project for 'Making Peace Perpetual in Europe', which was afterwards rewritten for all to read by Jean-Jacques Rousseau. But he also wrote a project for 'Making Roads Passable in Winter', and for the 'Reform of Begging'. Certainly his 'Project for Making Dukes and Peers Useful' was singularly optimistic.

In an age when most laws and customs were based on medieval beliefs and passed on unchanged from an obviously outworn social order, it was natural to assume that once good laws were passed, evil customs would disappear. The eighteenth century is the story of entrenched state and Church authority breaking down before the onslaught of the humanist attack, which may be said to have begun with Bacon and to have culminated in the French Revolution and the enthronement of the Goddess of Reason. The story is not confined to France, but had some parallels in many countries during the Enlightenment.

In England, for instance, our reformers had a similar, if less eloquent and enthusiastic faith. Jeremy Bentham also worked out rational solutions for all our problems; his disciples laid down the basis of middle-class reform and applied the theory of utility to every issue. Victorian England was their creation. Sometimes the simplicity of their arguments makes us laugh. James Mill, for example, argued that since each man best knew his own interests, democracy must serve society best; the majority must always govern better than the minority, while monarchy, serving only its own interests, must be the worst type of government. On similar grounds, after the middle-class victory of 1832, it was expected that all hereditary institutions would disappear, from beefeaters down to the House of Lords and the Monarchy; the Church of England would be disestablished, and all forms of privilege swept away as soon as every man and woman could write to M.P.s and understand the issues of the day by reading the newspapers. There would be no need for authority, the part played by religion would be taken over by science, and men, naturally reasonable, would cease to need kings, popes or priests and discover the good way of life for themselves.

Some of these assumptions are still made by many rationalists today. Liberals have held this view, with greater or less simplicity, and it lies behind most of our social legislation. The great differences between humanism in the eighteenth century and today are, first, that we no longer believe in a fixed 'natural law', but in evolutionary

81

change, and, and, secondly, that we are aware of man's unconscious and of the appalling difficulty of changing tradition and increasing the part that reason can play in society. The chief enemies of humanism are those who hold that revealed religion is a necessity, whether or not it is objectively true. The reaction against the gospel of Progress is of course powerful today, because science seems to be leading us not to Utopia, but to greater social misery, if not to the final solution of nuclear warfare.

II

Humanism seemed sure of victory before the 1914 war. The more history and memoirs I read, the clearer it becomes to me that 1914 was a great watershed in human thought. I note, for instance, that one of the most dogmatic of humanists recently remarked in his autobiography that when he was young, early in this century, there seemed no great evils in society to worry about. The Dreyfus case seemed to his generation a decisive victory of reason over reaction. Humanists, with Anatole France in the vanguard, defeated the Army, the anti-Semites, and all those who believed that justice was less important than the prestige of the established order. Until 1914 it seemed that democracy was spreading; that with the advance of education, rationalism would take the place of faith, that a man of liberal ideas could welcome the steady advance of happiness. Corruption had in fact grown less frequent with the advent of democracy; torture seemed a thing of the past; the welfare state had taken root, especially in Germany and England; international institutions of all kinds were increasingly common and effective. To H. G. Wells, for instance, the most imaginative of the apostles of progress, war had seemed out of date. He could speculate about fanciful struggles against Martians in hypothetical aircraft. But after 1919 he spent his life fighting to maintain what he thought already won. He had discovered from his own success as a propagandist that men were terribly gullible and far more nationalistic than he had thought. Under Northcliffe he had preached 'the war to end war' and had at first believed his own denunciation of Germany's unique wickedness; after the Kaiser's defeat there would be a chance of world government. When the smoke had been cleared, he saw that he had been exploited and had been persuaded to exploit young manhood; it had been driven into the slaughterhouse so that the nationalism he most hated would be more powerfully established. His task now was to teach mankind the basic tenets of humanism, whose victory he had assumed. People had to be taught the history of man's progress, the story of scientific advance, and the achievements and possibilities of social salvation. They must be educated, above all, in internationalism. Socialism was the logical outcome of science and democracy; they would see progress in terms of human advancement and not in those of individual success in the economic jungle. But in the end he despaired. Fascism and the Second World War were the final blow. Mind, he wrote in his old age when the bombs were falling, had 'reached the end of its tether'.

Wells of course was then old, and it was rather his own mind than mankind's that was exhausted. But it was true that the period in which men imagined that science was leading to Utopia was past, and that the age of enlightenment had given place to an era, first of scepticism, and finally of pessimism. Scientists were no longer sure about the predictability of the laws of physics and the social revolution seemed even more wayward. The story of the Russian Revolution had also brought disappointment. The last king, in Russia at least, had, as 18th century revolutionaries hoped, been 'strangled in the guts of the last priest', and the Soviet revolution had been as lavish as the French in promises of liberty, equality, and fraternity. Disappointment was all the greater when the actual outcome was the creation of another, even more ruthless, powerful, regimented and highly national state.

In 1963 we are again more hopeful of less nationalistic and more liberal trends in the U.S.S.R. But here I am only concerned with the excessive optimism of revolutionaries who again hoped to end ancient superstitions at a blow; and I recall that it was commonly said that the tyranny of pre-revolutionary Russia was based on two things—popular love for the Czar and faith in the Orthodox Church. The effect of their abolition in the two cases was quite different.

Take first the story of Monarchy since 1917. No one outside royal circles seemed much troubled by the murder of the Czar and his family. Czardom, tyranny and poverty went together, and Stalin could set up a more efficient and equally ruthless substitute. The need for

84

monarchy as an institution proved a myth. Monarchies fell in all but six countries in Europe, and ordinary people were quite happy about their disappearance. It is often held that the British monarchy has some peculiar character which gives it a permanent place in the lives of the people. It is true that it has been immensely popular and still maintains much of its hold because, unlike many other monarchies, it has surrendered its power and allows dissatisfaction with the government to find its outlet in dismissing the Prime Minister and not killing the King. But the myth that the British Commonwealth was essentially monarchist is shattered by the substitution of republics for what used to be British colonies. There is clearly nothing sacrosanct or permanent about the Crown. If Queen Victoria had not lived so long, and George V had not been able so successfully to appeal to his subjects, Britain might easily have become a republic like most other modern countries. There is still a weight of opinion in favour of the British monarchy, and it will last while the occupants of the Throne are of good character and do not interfere with politics. But it has become what Mr Muggeridge has rightly called an *ersatz* religion. Once essential, monarchies have become increasingly mere survivals of the hereditary system. It is doubtful whether the opponents of humanism would today argue that the House of Lords has a deep psychological hold on public imagination. Though the popularity of the monarchy is strong, I don't think any humanist need be bothered if he is twitted with being a republican. Whether he decides that it is politically expedient to advocate republicanism is quite another question. It may well be more convenient to have a monarch than a president, and a queen may be more popular than the presidents of France or America. But today the decision is, like others, one of expediency. It depends on circumstances and the character of individuals who occupy the throne.

Compare this story with the Marxian attack on religion. Many rationalists assumed that the anti-God campaign in Russia would get rid of the Church just as effectively as the revolutionaries had ended Czardom. The Church was corrupt, money-grubbing and relied on faked miracles. Its exposure was complete; the state funds on which the Church depended were withdrawn and many churches were shut. It proved untrue, however, that only the older generation would remain pious. Even today, after forty-five years, the many surviving churches are well-attended, and on Church festivals I have seen thousands thronging to Communion. Beneath their breath millions are still 'believers'. It is clearly untrue that all the younger generation will be uninterested in the ceremonials and doctrines of Orthodoxy; many who worship today were young in the early days of the Revolution. In the war Stalin found it necessary deliberately to enlist the aid of the Church, and it remains today part of the state apparatus. In so far as it goes, Soviet experience provides evidence of Jung's archetypes. The Trinity and the gospel story satisfy a craving which is not readily met by state pageantry and rational doctrine. There is nothing here to guide us in our attempts to answer the question whether men can be satisfied everywhere without revealed religion.

The third lesson from Soviet experience is also important. If history is largely the result of class conflict, and the classes themselves are the result of economic forces in society, it easily follows that most men's opinions are dictated by their economic status. Marxists have gone to greater lengths than other socialists (with the exception perhaps of Robert Owen) in believing that you can determine opinion by changing circumstances. If you give the peasant the land he will become more than ever an individualist. If by a combination of force and other inducements you make him a member of a commune, cultivating in co-operation with others, with obvious economic advantages, it could be easily assumed that the individualist peasant would become a communist. Nothing of the sort has occurred. I recall visiting Peking in 1955 and congratulating a company of Chinese officials on Chinese common sense in not repeating Stalin's mistake of forcible communalization; how much wiser China was to rely on gradual co-operation by example! A smile began to appear on every face; it was quickly wiped off because in those days to admit gratification at the expense of the Soviet Union was not correct. Since then the Chinese have reversed their policy and introduced collective agriculture, with the usual bad effects on production. Agricultural communes have had to be widely and generally abandoned in the communist world. The peasant's relation to his land is not at all similar to the industrial worker's attitude to the conveyor belt. Like the Russians, the Chinese have succeeded far beyond anyone's expectations in industrial progress, but have discovered that peasants do not become communists by being pushed into communes.

We may summarize the story so far. First, rationalists have been wrong in assuming that an institution must disappear when its irrationality is exposed. It was by no means certain, for instance, that a religion would disappear because people could no longer believe in many of the myths and institutions in which it was traditionally embodied. People may continue to hold irrational opinions because subconsciously they wish to, and rationalists may be attacking spurious arguments, ignorant of the true supports of the institution they are attacking. Secondly, though economic factors and political institutions are certainly important in moulding opinions, it is rash to assume that there are not other factors equally, or even more, powerful. Thirdly, it is no longer clear that the progress of science means the progress of mankind.

A book like Aldous Huxley's *Brave New World* suggested that science could be used, not to liberate, but to enslave men and women. Rulers might be able, with the help of scientific propaganda, to dominate, perhaps even to destroy, the minds of the mass of men and women. Again, and more immediately, science has already added a further threat to progress by vastly increasing the world's population. Doctors have made great strides towards death-control, but are only now on the way to finding inexpensive and available methods of birth-control. Finally, science has discovered a means of world destruction. We are exposed to a double threat. Unless an agreement is reached between the nuclear powers, the 'population explosion', by which the world will be twice as heavily populated by the end of the century, may be finally solved by a nuclear war.

III

We have to face the world drift to disaster. For drift it is. There is today no world policy or deliberate direction. No one can say, as we did half a century ago, that having repudiated the medieval picture of a celestial paradise mankind has decided to march forwards to a heaven on earth. The question is whether those who are capable of understanding the dangers can unite and work together to reverse the downhill trend. They are no longer obliged, or indeed able, to hold that science is leading to Utopia, any more than their opponents any longer believe in paradise. What they have to demonstrate is that our problems can be dealt with rationally and that progress is still possible. We have the right, in my view, to claim that humanism can still point the way to a better society and better human beings. If we do not make the mistake of promising unlimited improvement and uninterrupted progress, we can still establish our credentials.

How much can the humanist claim for his modest non-Utopian approach? About the nuclear threat we can assert that our future depends on shedding inherited prejudices and national habits of thought. We no longer believe in the God of Wrath, but the creation of a scientific god will not in itself save us. Men can end their society with ideological slogans on their lips as well as with national ones. We can, however, proclaim that the solution, which must surely be some form of world government, is not likely as the result of military victory of one class over others.

Similarly, to defeat the menace of over-population, superstitious objections to birth-control must be swallowed; otherwise the prospect is that the world will get rapidly poorer and more violent. No longer will the prospect of immortality compensate for the miseries of this world. Many will deplore the loss of faith in immortality, but today few believe it in the same sense that they believe that by catching the 8.05 in the morning they will reach the office by 9.00 a.m. Assertions about the world beyond the grave are increasingly a pretence, born of the difficulty of facing our own extinction and the desperate desire to meet again those that we have lost. All that we can say is that life here can be happier for our children and successors if we learn and practise the laws of well-being.

Once we have accepted the fact that the world here is as we ourselves make it, our problem becomes one of human behaviour. How far, if at all, we can change *human nature* we do not know, but we have plenty of evidence that we can change *behaviour* for the better, even though the process is less simple and less dependent on obvious improvements of physical circumstance than we imagined. Here we are perhaps on the threshold of new knowledge; because of ancient dogmas the understanding of the human mind is, deplorably, the latest and least surely investigated of human sciences. It is the next door that must be opened. Mankind's future is infinitely more dependent on our knowledge of the human mind than on our success in travelling in outer space and reaching the distant stars.

So we come back to morality, that is, to the way men treat each other.

Marriage provides an excellent illustration of the fight between humanists and the Church. Historically speaking, marriage is supported by a long Jewish and Christian tradition, and its alternative was assumed to be 'free love'. In fact, of course, the institution of marriage was based not on clerical doctrine or biblical texts, but on society's need to ensure inheritance, to give security to women when they were wholly dependent on men, and to provide some curb for the most tempestuous of human passions. With the improvements in methods of birth-control and the emancipation of women, marriage became less essential and a new sexual code developed. This code has long been well accepted, in Scandinavia for instance; even in Britain it is commonly practised though still officially repudiated. Briefly, its principles are that sex relations must be subject to two conditions: first, it is always wrong for one human being to exploit another, sexually as in other ways. This condemns prostitution and all sex relations which are not born of love. The second principle is that to bring a child into the world is a grave matter for which the state must hold man and woman alike responsible. These principles are not anarchic; on the contrary, if observed, they form the basis for a firm family life and will inevitably be accepted by honourable people. They do not exclude extra-marital relations. The trap for the unwary humanist is that he may talk as if marriage is unimportant, and forget that one of its main supports is that it does something to control the jealousy which is the common accompaniment of genuine passion. People in love often want to be bound to each other, not free. One needs little more than ordinary knowledge of human behaviour to understand why communities in which people try to share everything, even love affairs, have not been successful, and why many people who begin by boasting of their emancipation have been disillusioned when they have tried to put their theories into practice. Bertrand Russell, in the remarkable essays he wrote about social reconstruction after the First World War, spoke with perhaps delusive clarity on the subject; we should, however, welcome his dictum, accepted so often in theory rather than practice by the emancipated, that 'jealousy is a worse sin than adultery'.

Marriage provides a striking example of the way in which the Church loses ground by failing to concentrate on the basic human problem; it prefers to stress the Scriptures, pronouncing anathemas and pretending that the traditional forms are the only basis for respectability. The result of this persistent, and indeed desperate clutching at the past is that the Church has constantly to find subterfuges for accepting the facts of society.

The Church of England, for instance, has at last been compelled to sanction birth-control, and as the frightening truth about the growth of the world population and its relation to poverty becomes clear, the pressure on the Catholic Church to find theological loopholes also becomes great within its own increasingly disobedient flock. I am told today that many well-to-do Catholics in the United States now receive dispensations from their confessors to use contraceptives. It is in any case accepted that birth-control is commonly practised by Catholics, and the arguments about whether any method outside the entirely insecure 'safe period' can be permitted have become so tortuous that any reader of Roman Catholic pamphlets on the subject is justified in misunderstanding them.

The Vatican has indeed plunged into a quagmire by arguing that the human embryo must have a soul, so that it is murder to prevent a child being born. But at what point, as Voltaire asked two hundred years ago, does God insert the soul into the foetus? Will it, perhaps—and many humane and intelligent priests now ask themselves this—be found good Catholic doctrine that a contraceptive pill, by preventing conception, is somehow more permissible than a chemical or mechanical device? And what if there is a choice between the life of the mother and of the child? At what point is abortion ever permissible? It is clearly not enough to say that doctors must always do their best to preserve both lives; sometimes a deliberate choice has to be made and a risk to be run. Are doctors to be condemned for quietly deciding not to keep monsters and hopelessly defective babies alive when they are born? And is it anything but hypocrisy for a doctor to refuse an operation because he is a Catholic, knowing, in fact, that he has left the act of killing to a Protestant friend?

It must be obvious to everyone that decisions in all these matters will ultimately be utilitarian. The appeal to a religious tradition or sacrosanct phrase from Holy Writ may retard rational policy or lead to tortuous argument, but we know— none better than the ecclesiastical authorities— that in the long run policy must be based on the daily needs of this century. It is dangerous as well as absurd to rely on Authority when it is no longer generally accepted. Morality is not strengthened but weakened by the backing of such doctrines as the Virgin Birth, the Resurrection, or the Assumption. An instructive example is to be found in Mr Norman St John Stevas's book, *The Right to Live*. A lawyer and a Catholic, he discusses the problems of life and death raised by thalidomide babies, by suicide, birth-control, abortion, capital punishment and military conscription. In every case he starts from the Christian view of the sanctity of human life, supported by the Old Testament commandment against killing and by such remarks as that God gave man dominion over animals; he then goes on to explain why society and the Churches, in fact favour killing when convenient.

The whole picture of society has been completely changed by the pioneers of science, anthropology, psychology and history. Darwin, Marx, Fraser and Freud were none of them infallible, but they have taught us to think in a way that excludes the story that mankind began

94

four thousand and four years ago in the Garden of Eden; that we were created by a God of Wrath and Mercy who gave man the chance to sin and go to hell unless he accepted redemption through the sacrificial death of his only-begotten son. These words are worth repeating even though they sound ridiculous today, because hundreds of sermons are preached in churches and on the radio, numerous books, papers and arguments are based on them; though very few believe them, it is still considered improper to make fun of them.

The one serious argument for continuing to use them in our places of worship is that they have psychological value even though they may not have objective truth. In short it is argued that there is no need to fight against revealed religion because almost all educated people already reject it except in some symbolic sense. The chief objection to this argument is that this retention of out-of-date form interferes with the deliberate and general teaching of the evolutionary story, which in general terms is now universally accepted. The pretence of believing mythology makes it difficult to face public issues realistically. We are in danger of creating a society in which an educated and scientifically-minded élite itself rejects a body of teaching which is maintained for the supposedly ignorant and unenlightened masses. The result is hypocrisy, and a dangerous and unstable social confusion. It would be foolish to imagine that in countries like Spain and Portugal, for instance, the cardinals and bishops, the ministers and officials share the ignorance they endeavour to maintain by propaganda, censorship and, above all, by retaining an absolute control over education. Such a system can only survive in a totalitarian regime.

I was once involved in a most instructive controversy with a clergyman who wrote a long and able letter to *The New Statesman and Nation* about the dangers of discarding the transcendental element in religion. He argued that the rejection of theological doctrine was leading to looseness of ethical principle and that people like myself who held moral principles, but rejected their theological foundation, were unable to speak with authority or pass on our own high ethical standards. I had been brought up, he argued, by parents who believed in goodness and knew why; but because I had rejected revealed religion, I was like a mule who could not pass on his inheritance to any offspring. *The New Statesman* would never become Fascist as long as it was run by people like myself, but I could not explain to the younger generation why they should not practice torture or live purely pleasure-seeking lives. I was in effect free-wheeling off my father and incapable of carrying the younger generation with me.

In answer to this there seemed to me several conclusive points to make. First, I do not believe that morality depends on belief in any set of theological doctrines; it is statistically true that people do not behave better because they hold long-established doctrines. A high proportion of the criminal classes in England, for instance, go to Mass and confess their sins. The countries in which Fascism most easily gained control were those with the highest proportion of devout Catholics. It is not an accident that the home of Fascism was Italy, and that resistance in Spain came chiefly from anti-clericals, or that in Germany and elsewhere the Catholic Church made no effective resistance to Hitlerism. Secondly, the reasons for moral behaviour seem to be primarily utilitarian; where moral standards decline the reason would seem to be that the whole social synthesis of a society breaks up. Thirdly, the morality accepted in any society does not depend on the Churches (which broadly agree everywhere on what constitutes good behaviour) but on the basic needs of a civilized society. The reason for talking of the fatherhood of God is the social necessity of the brotherhood of man. That, fundamentally, is what is at stake in all racialism. It is so disastrous in its social results, though defended with peculiar intensity by the most religious section of white people in South Africa, that to combat it has become one of the clearest of moral duties. So it is with each accepted doctrine; it is a poetic way of giving authority to principles that ultimately depend on utility. Once the mass of people realize that Church doctrines are not based on objective truth, they cannot be maintained; and teaching must be substituted that accords with the knowledge we have, coupled with the proviso that the new explanation will also be modified with new knowledge. All fixed authority is a casualty in an evolutionary age. Finally, it is astonishing to me to find religious persons arguing in favour of orthodox beliefs, not because they are true but because they fear the results of rejecting them.

The one point of importance still made in the plea for an orthodox God is, I think, that a large proportion of mankind desire an authority, crave for an authoritarian religion and are deeply unhappy if they lack more than ordinary human assurance. I recall a conversation with the daughter of highly educated atheist parents. She said that if she didn't believe that Christ had died for her and that happiness waited after death she would find life impossible and commit suicide. On another occasion, a young Roman Catholic of great ability, who obviously did not believe in the doctrines of his Church, frankly said that if I were determined to seek truth I should no doubt remain an agnostic and find life difficult; if I wanted contentment and an easy mind it was a good idea to accept Catholicism. He talked as if you could choose what you believed. To me this is mysterious, because the notion of deliberately believing things is meaningless.

The existence of a 'God-shaped hole' inside a large number of people does not mean that we cannot have a society without an authoritarian religion. Jung and others have, I think, shown that there is a correspondence between our mental inheritance and religious doctrines such as the Trinity. Such doctrines continue to exist because they correspond to archetypes. The desire to believe continues even when the objective fact is disregarded. Yet many people manage quite well without transcendental religion and an increasing number share a scientific outlook which demands a suspension of belief. The fact that Jung sometimes found it helpful to restore the faith of patients who had nervous breakdowns does not prove that most of us need have either nervous breakdowns or faith. What I think it does suggest is that rationalists tend too often to throw out the baby with the bath-water.

The habit of prayer provides a valuable example. Any intelligent child today learns that there is not a father in heaven who gives you presents because you ask for them. Most set prayers are now quite indefensible. We have given up expecting God to arrange rain or fine weather for our convenience, and we do not expect our armies to defeat other armies because our churches are fuller than those of our enemies; nor is it anything but nauseating to pretend that our soldiers will succeed in killing their enemies while they themselves will be immune from bullets because their relatives are saying the right thing to God. Many people continue to derive comfort from praying for the recovery of sick relatives, but few of them, I think, really believe that some mysterious personality is listening to their words and will interfere with the normal course of a disease in answer to a special request. All this is so clear that prayer has become largely a formality. It has, however, another use which is commonly disregarded in our rationalist age. It may help us to avoid the tyranny of chance desires. Prayer may be the concentration of mind upon purposes which are more likely to be fulfilled if clearly formulated and deliberately repeated. The West has forgotten the value of meditation. I strongly suspect that many people would be happier and more faithful to their vows and intentions if they understood the value of a habit which often degenerates into mere hypocrisy.

IV

If we summarize this story we find a process widely operating in society. All institutions eventually grow out of date: they demand the acceptance of doctrines that science contradicts and loyalties which thoughtful people cannot give. When that happens the rationalist, testing the institution by its utility and credibility, attacks it and easily assumes that the world will be better for abolishing another piece of mumbo-jumbo. It may then be found that it has served a purpose not usually understood by the upholders of the mumbo-jumbo. A reaction takes place and the institution continues to be both defended and attacked on the wrong grounds. If other ways are found of fulfilling the real purpose of the institution it will die, though mumbo-jumbo will continue to be muttered for a long time. This is the case, for instance, in all controversies about hereditary institutions. No one will really bother if we substitute a rational Second Chamber for the House of Lords, and the institution of monarchy is similarly on the way out. But the case of revealed religion is not in my view parallel. A large proportion of people feel that they need some assurance outside themselves. Many who no longer believe in any revealed authority desire the solid assurance of public and familiar ceremonial. It has always been a weakness of rationalism that it has found no way of satisfying the desire for the communal expression of emotion. People feel the need of a ritual and of traditional words on the occasions of birth, marriage and death.

Because this craving for ceremonial is still strong in many, but, I think, a decreasing number of people, the humanist does not expect quickly to satisfy those whom William James called the tender-minded. He can, however, say with confidence that a far larger number of people are humanists today than care to admit it and that much good would be done if they were more candid. Similarly it is the humanist's duty to state his faith in positive form. We have no right to stand on the sidelines and scoff at the irrationality of other people. The fight against entrenched orthodoxy has been so long and bitter that we have grown too satisfied with polemics.

A negative attitude has been easy because it has long been clear that many who go to church have ceased to believe their own words. Some cling to the familiar phrases because they have found in their private interpretations an aid to a satisfactory life. For the most part, however, religion is formal and the dominant faith of western society in the last century has been belief in the material improvement of mankind on earth combined with the assumption of a concomitant spiritual improvement. If we recall the names of those we all revere as deserving mankind's greatest praise, we do not find that most of them have been believers. Mainly they have been those who have deepened and broadened knowledge, or increased happiness through their understanding of the present world. Most of our creative writers, artists and poets have ceased to find their inspiration in the doctrines of the Churches. The concern of thinking people is with the health, wealth and happiness of mankind. Our job is the well-being of men and the hoped-for peace among nations. The obstacles in our way are far greater than our forefathers imagined, but if society breaks up, it will not be because we do not believe in revealed religion but because we fail to solve our mundane problems. Men are more nationalistic, violent and stupid than they thought they were. We control the earth and the air, but not the tiger, the ape and the donkey inside ourselves.

The humanist faith is that reason can play a decisive role and that religious doctrines are for the most part obstructive. We hold that our acceptance of evolution and of science as a key to knowledge makes it morally wrong, and indeed hypocritical, to repeat antiquated phrases; that the first principle of valid social thinking is that nothing is known for certain and that we should act on the best knowledge we have and only on that. We have good reason to believe in the possibility of far greater happiness if society pays attention to ethical principles that follow from the needs of our common humanity. Humanism is an attitude of mind. Some may even find in it the inspiration of a religion. It enables them to see themselves and their society in perspective, and provides a working theory of life which is consistent with current scientific knowledge. It becomes a duty, not only a sensible line of conduct, to work for a world society and dedicate our lives to the still rational hope of progress. The future depends on ourselves, not on any doctrine. We may believe that men progress, not towards Utopia or perfectibility, but towards a happier and more reasonable society.

The Pointlessness of it All

H. J. BLACKHAM

Is Humanism a Nihilism?

THE most drastic objection to humanism is that it is too bad to be true. The world is one vast tomb if human lives are ephemeral and human life itself doomed to ultimate extinction. There is head-on opposition here from all developed religions, which say: the eternal alone; the temporal redeemed by the eternal; never, the temporal alone.

How nihilistic is humanism? There is no question here of a metaphysical doctrine, 'refusing a substantial reality to the phenomenal existence of which we are conscious', for this has no practical consequences, except to show up 'the whimsical condition of mankind'. Moral scepticism, however, which can only ask, 'What is the use?' and find no answer, and may be violent and destructive or bored and indolent, has some relevance to humanism, for although neither the violence nor boredom characteristic of nihilism is characteristic of humanists, the question is, why not? Nietzsche, having decided that God is dead, knew with vertigo that he danced on the edge of the abyss; and not until he felt he could embrace the most senseless and repulsive possibility—Eternal Recurrence of the same meaningless sequence—did he feel safe ground under his feet. Another more recent attempt to take seriously the consequences of humanist assumptions is Bertrand Russell's 'A Free Man's Worship':

> That Man is the product of causes which had no prevision of the end they were achieving; that his origin, his growth, his hopes and fears, his loves and his beliefs, are but the outcome of accidental collocations of atoms; that no fire, no heroism, no intensity of thought and feeling, can preserve an individual life beyond the grave; that all the labour of the ages, all the devotion, all the inspiration, all the noonday brightness of human genius, are destined to extinction in the vast death of the solar system, and that the whole temple of Man's achievement must inevitably be buried beneath the debris of a universe in ruins—all these things, if not quite beyond dispute, are yet so nearly certain, that no philosophy which rejects them can hope to stand. Only within the scaffolding of these truths, only on the firm

foundation of unyielding despair, can the soul's habitation henceforth be safely built.

It is too true to be good: let us acknowledge the truth, and provide the goodness ourselves, with pride and without hope.

One answer to the objection, then, is this: humanists are concerned primarily with the truth of the human situation; if in fact it is gloomy, and they have to build on despair or the other side of despair, so be it; at least they can build, and do not have to turn bored and indolent or violent and destructive. Nihilism does not follow logically from humanist premises. Neither value nor the negation of value can be an inference from fact. Of course, what does not follow logically may tend to follow psychologically, what is not required by reason may be very reasonable. 'Living on Christian capital' is an objection not to be shoved aside by the irritation it naturally provokes.

There is another way of looking at this. If one starts from the Christian point of view, humanism is merely an exercise in vital subtraction: God goes, the soul goes, sin and death remain; the outlook becomes extremely bleak. The humanist must agree. If he took his Christian friend along to a performance of *Hamlet* without the Prince of Denmark to point out the beauties that remained, he would not expect this to go down as though it were *Hamlet* in modern dress. There is a type of humanist who *is* a Christian *manqué*, who may manage to endure to the end; but he is not representative. Nor is the humanist the fox without a tail; if he has no tail, it is because he is a different breed of fox. He is not looking at the Christian world without faith and hope. He has turned completely round and sees another scene. He starts with positive acceptance and appreciation of the conditions of the natural world, and gladly gathers the perishable happiness that is to be had and enjoyed.

We create the world we live in by our expectations and attitudes, our ideas and ideals, and the ways in which we interpret and manage our experience. The humanist is not a Christian stripped of his Christian expectations, attitudes, ideas, ideals, and techniques of living: he is a man with a different equipment. As Wordsworth recognized in the arts, new work has to create the taste by which it is to be enjoyed, and then it becomes its own standard. We look for what is not there and are blind to what is there. Christians and humanists inhabit different worlds and have to do violence to what has become their own nature to understand one another, to stop looking at things as they do, to stop seeing what they see. This is almost too much to ask. Because they have grown apart in different worlds, discussion between Christians and humanists is seldom profitable. All the more reason to make the most of an opportunity like this when a few Christians and humanists are prepared to take unusually seriously some of the persistent objections to their positions.

An historical view

Long before Christ, the elegiac note on human experience was heard:

108

Not to be born at all is the happiest lot for mortal,
Never to open eyelids on the bright shafts of the sun:
Or, born, as soon as may be to pass beyond Death's portal,
To draw earth's heavy mantle above him, and have done.   (Theognis.)

An extreme view of course, but the Wisdom literature in the Bible is hardly more favourable.

A therapeutic view of man's case was taken by Stoics and Epicureans, 'the two most celebrated sects in the world and the only rational ones', as Pascal observed to his confessor. They were the only rational ones because they took up the two mutually exclusive and exhaustive alternatives: God exists, and the sovereign good for humanity is found only in conformity to his will; or God's existence is uncertain—with different possible consequences. (Here Pascal, fascinated by Montaigne's scepticism, failed to appreciate the strength of the position of Epicurus who dogmatically denied any concern of the gods with human life, and any survival of death.)

Stoics and Epicureans had agreed in saying that man had his cure in his own hands, although they had radically disagreed on diagnosis and prescription. Pascal, as a good Christian, agreed that man was sick, but could not agree that he could cure himself. The Stoic or Epicurean sage was not the natural human being: he had to make himself at home in the world by a concentrated exercise of will and reason. For him, the whole of life was learning to live and learning to die. The

Christian saint, on the other hand, neither schooled himself to indifference nor cultivated the husbandry of wise choice and avoidance to remain at home in the world, but, knowing that his home was elsewhere, gladly increased his portion of suffering and service here. The men of the Renaissance were not interested in the programme of the sage nor in 'monkish virtues', for they had rediscovered the novelty of everything under the sun and were immersed in the active business and leisure of life in its immediacy and miscellaneity. Nor were the men who behaved thus just average sensual men of any time or place whom you could not compare with the elect of any school. Like Stoics and Epicureans, they were men of reflection, but had come to the conclusion that man is not to be placed above and out of life by the discipline of reason and will. Without disavowing Christianity, they broke with the therapeutic view of man.

For Pomponazzi (1462–1524), man exercises nis thought in contact with the perishable and by means of the perishable, and is himself perishable; he cannot go out of himself, he is not a stranger in the world, he is bound to it by his mind, not merely by his body. Nostalgia, desire, cannot enter into the question; the world as it is found is the measure. Man is what he is by the whole manner of being inherent in his species: immortality is out of the question—except of course that it is revealed to faith. Man in and of this world, however, is called to the moral task which life together in this world imposes on humanity. Pomponazzi's humanism stands here in contrast with the religious platonism of Ficino and Pico,

for whom the soul's nostalgia for another world
is the intimation of its immortality. After the
total domination of Christendom by ecclesiastical thinking in the Middle Ages, the two
types, humanist and religious, reappear in an
ambiguous context: man is only at home in this
world; he is never at home here.

In Petrarca and Erasmus, unquestionably good
Christians, life as lived and felt by all, rather than
as thought by the philosopher, comes into its own:
the human domain is man's *patrie*, and his
delight. Let a man accept himself as he finds
himself, and explore what is open to him. Each
has his own way of being human. No one can
be more than a man. The concreteness of shared
humanity and experience was as exciting and
far-reaching a discovery as the New World and,
later, the new knowledge. In the Enlightenment,
the Christian humanism of Erasmus triumphed
over the Lutheran and Calvinistic sense of utter
dependence on God, with its tendency to anni-
hilate the humanity of man by diminishing its
status. 'All this and heaven too' or, in Jefferson's
phrase, 'Happiness on earth and greater happiness hereafter', was a complacent creed. But
the notion of having to do without Part Two
gained ground, and was accepted with fortitude
as part of man's maturity—not for the first
time.

The purpose of this glance at 'philosophical
anthropology' is to recall the persistence in
different contexts down the ages of two clear-cut
theories, the one prescribing for man on his own
in this world which is all he has and ever will have,
the other prescribing for the pilgrim and alien

forbidden to make his home here. Between these parallels runs the line of those who refuse to force the issue, content to make the best of this world in high hopes of the next, or with diminished or vanished hopes. The humanist can be put on trial for reducing human life to pointlessness, because the evidence can be brought into court and may lead to a verdict against him. The Christian cannot be put on trial, since there is no conclusive evidence in his case. But if he stakes his whole life on his belief and is deceived, that might be a model of pointlessness, although it could never be proved. Let him remember his immunity, rather than his innocence, when he brings this objection against the humanist.

Values and conditions

Now, a glance along a different line of inquiry: what are the general conditions which incline people to find life good, and those which induce revolt or disgust?

The most savage comment ever put into words is put into the mouth of one who has 'supp'd full with horrors', whose conscience is loaded with guilt, who has alienated himself from golden opinions and troops of friends, who has staked heavily and forfeited all: 'Tomorrow, and to-morrow, and tomorrow . . . it is a tale Told by an idiot, full of sound and fury, Signifying nothing' (*Macbeth*, Act V, scene v). Crime, vaulting ambition, does not make a sane witness. The evidence of those who have plunged into excesses speaks only of the worth of their aims.

The excesses of actual crime are hardly distinguishable psychologically from the excesses of romantic egoism. Take Chateaubriand as the type, and the letter of René to his wife Celuta in *Les Natchez* as the example:

> Celuta, there are existences so tempestuous that they seem to accuse Providence and would cure one of the mania of being. From the beginning of my life I have not ceased to nourish sorrows; I carried the germs of them in myself as the tree bears the germs of its fruit. An unknown poison mingled with all my feelings. . . . I suppose, Celuta, that René's heart now opens before you: do you see the extraordinary world it contains? From this heart rise flames which lack food, which would devour creation without being satiated, which would devour yourself. . . .

Sainte-Beuve, having quoted this passage, comments: 'That instinctive and universal feeling which makes life seem sweet and dear to every mortal, even in misfortune, which makes all creatures, when once born into the world, to love and regret *the sweet light of day*, he calls a mania'. Sainte-Beuve goes on to trace this interfusion of sensual pleasure with the idea of death and annihilation, and quotes Chateaubriand again (for he is aiming at the author himself), in the words of the dying Atala to Chactas:

> . . . sometimes I could have wished to be with you the only living creature on earth; sometimes, feeling a divine prompting which would check me in my horrible transports, I could have wished that this divinity might be annihilated, so long as, locked in your arms, I

113

might have rolled from abyss to abyss with the ruins of God and the world.

This rage of destruction and self-destruction is characteristic of romantic excess, and excess is characteristic of the romantic. Yet he is one of the last to lose faith in life. 'It is part of his inspiration to believe that he creates a new heaven and a new earth with each revolution in his moods or in his purposes. He ignores, or seeks to ignore, all the conditions of life . . .' (Santayana: *Three Philosophical Poets*, p. 144). He has a philosophy of life that often sees him through. 'To live, to live just as we do, that is the purpose and the crown of living. . . . The worth of life lies in pursuit, not in attainment; therefore everything is worth pursuing, and nothing brings satisfaction— save this endless destiny itself.' At the end, he can say without disenchantment: 'I have felt'.

Illusion is possible to the will, even the will to will, the indefinite idealism of the romantic. It is not possible to the brooding introspective intelligence which drags everything out of the sun to scrutinize it under the pale cast of thought. Amiel is a beautiful example. Matthew Arnold, no philosopher, brushed aside with the impatience of a sensible man all that is most characteristic of Amiel, and called attention to the excellent literary critic the world had lost in this lost soul sterile with unprofitable yearnings for the infinite, neglecting a true vocation. Healthy-minded dismissal of Amiel's brain-sick musings in the manner of Arnold is fair enough. For Amiel shows very well, not least to himself, one not uncommon way of making oneself unfit to live. But Amiel was not teaching anybody anything, save, very gently, that it is best not to quarrel with any illusion and to treat life as the grandfather treats his grand-daughter. He peered and stared into the bottom of his questions, and a course of Amiel would do no harm to anyone who is prepared to try to bear to live without illusions, warned that there are more illusions in heaven and earth than are dreamt of in any philosophy, however sceptical.

There is perhaps a normal sequence in the development of sensibility, which is seen in heightened representation in Wordsworth. First comes the flush of sensations in childhood, a magnet for later recollections, when the world 'did seem Apparell'd in celestial light'. Then 'the coarser pleasures', the 'glad animal movements', the bounding response of boyish days, forgotten when all natural sounds and forms and colours become 'an appetite, a feeling and a love' and yield aching joys and dizzy raptures, steadied by the dawn of ideal visions when to be young is very heaven. But the glory passes away from the earth, the visionary gleam vanishes, nostalgia remains, and petrified substitutes: recollections, images, fellow feeling, duty, faith. The loss of power, of vitality and imaginative response, may be sudden and complete, verging on collapse, or an ebb which leaves some trickle in the ruts and routines of daily rounds. Wordsworth's poetry during some ten years is a glorious attempt to recreate lost vitality through the natural images with which it was associated. This poetry, the cult of Nature as a substitute religion, helped probably many more than John Stuart Mill to gain or regain at a mature level some imaginative and emotional power, some colours and shapes beyond the uniform line and tone of duty and doctrine. No doubt the poet suffers for his hypersensibility, but Wordsworth speaks for more than himself. It may be folly to hope to improve 'transient Gleams of Joy . . . into an inviolable and perpetual State of Bliss and Happiness' (Addison), but who can bear to lose altogether the mind's 'auxiliar light' which transfigured the natural world; who can really find in his heart that Duty or Faith is the right and proper consolation for loss of vital power?

Perhaps not many are poets, even mute and inglorious, and it is not the inner loss of sensibility that strikes most people down, but, rather, the external strokes of misfortune. So long as all goes swimmingly there is nothing to trouble belief nor unbelief, but if and when the blows fall thick and fast enough, as on Job, religious faith is to be taken seriously or put seriously in question. Superior souls, like the Buddha or St Francis, do not have to wait for personal afflictions. They see all around abundant evidence that 'Life is a state in which much is to be endured, and little to be enjoyed'. The state of uneasiness, however induced, and it is commonly a sense of guilt and not merely misfortune, calls for a remedy and a prevention, and this, if it is a religious remedy, is at first a judgement of what is wrong, a self-judgement of the individual which is the beginning of self-transcendence, a consciousness of and an identification of himself with a higher part of the self—according to William James's generalization from case-studies of the variety of religious experience:

He becomes conscious that this higher part is conterminous and continuous with a MORE of the same quality, which is operative in the universe outside of him, and which he can keep in working touch with, and in a fashion get on board of and save himself when all his lower being has gone to pieces in the wreck. (*The Varieties of Religious Experience*. Lecture XX.)

This is a general statement of 'the perennial philosophy', the persistent religious philosophy to which men return generation after generation to find meaning for their lives. Granted that one is living in a fool's paradise unless and until one's eyes are opened to the real extent of human wretchedness (including the shabbiness under the surface), is 'the perennial philosophy' the only kind of thinking which can restore meaning to the world and make it acceptable?

Those who are inclined to answer yes to this question should not allow themselves to slip into thinking that this is a way out of responsibility for managing a meaningful existence in this world. And those who confidently say no to the question should not absurdly underestimate the difficulty of this management for 'an intellectual animal, and therefore an everlasting contradiction to himself' (Hazlitt).

Samuel Johnson, who wrote *The Vanity of Human Wishes* and knew the taste of exhausted despair, is one of the best examples of one who grasped the conditions on which human desires can be educated in the pursuit of their objects, and so satisfied, '*increasing* both the breadth and the durability of what is desired'. Of course

Johnson was a staunch Christian in a time of much falling away. He had been converted by Law's *Serious Call to a Devout and Holy Life*, which was a call to take Christianity very seriously indeed. No doubt his faith answered deeply to his needs, not least his obsessional fear of death and extinction, for he was often heard quoting to himself the passage in *Paradise Lost*, beginning,

for who would lose,
Though full of pain, this intellectual being.

But faith did not come first: 'Whether to see life as it is, will give us much consolation, I know not; *but the consolation which is drawn from truth, if any there be, is solid and durable;* that which may be derived from errour, must be, like its original, fallacious and fugitive'.[1] The stability of truth and the use of the mind in the management of a total experience are cardinal and permanent conditions of living to some purpose, of maintaining interest and zest, of not being tired of life even when one is tired of London.

Without looking any more closely at life or literature, one may dare to say summarily that the nuptial bond with the natural world can be formed and maintained with good luck and good care. To put down roots in this world, to give hostages to fortune, to multiply affections, attachments, associations, contrary to the prudence of those who would forestall fortunes and anticipate the worst, is the best way to reduce the feeling that we are such stuff as dreams are made on.

[1] See *The Achievement of Samuel Johnson*, by Walter Jackson Bate, A Galaxy Book.

The real objection

However, it can be said that the point of the objection has been lost in these digressions into theories of life and the phenomena of experience. There is no end to hiding from the ultimate end of life, which is death. But it does not avail. On humanist assumptions, life leads to nothing, and every pretence that it does not is a deceit. If there is a bridge over a gorge which spans only half the distance and ends in mid-air, and if the bridge is crowded with human beings pressing on, one after another they fall into the abyss. The bridge leads nowhere, and those who are pressing forward to cross it are going nowhere. It does not matter where they think they are going, what preparations for the journey they may have made, how much they may be enjoying it all. The objection merely points out objectively that such a situation is a model of futility.

Thus Heidegger insists that death is the capital fact in the light of which human existence is to be interpreted. Men find themselves cast into the world to die. This is their inescapable destiny, the true meaning of all lives. It is the absolute point of view for human beings, from which everything is to be seen and judged, for the look of things from any other point of view is illusionary. Human life may be absurd from this point of view, but it is absurd to look at it from any other point of view.

Is death the inescapable absolute, the only relevant consideration, or is it reasonable to take death as only one of the facts of life?

Obviously, there are relevant considerations

that would discount the absolute power of death. The truth of the Christian faith is one such consideration. Indeed, any assumption of a cosmic purpose such that whatever is is best (the view of the Stoics or of Hegel, for example) would discount death in this way. Such an assumption involves a double act of faith and reduces the good human possibilities to the fulfilment of the supposed non-human purpose. Nevertheless, on this assumption death is not capital and human life is redeemed from futility.

There is another assumption on which death is of negligible significance, namely, if everything were blindly determined, informed by no purpose nor meaning, and allowing no room for the kind of determinism and meaning introduced by human purposes. If human beings cannot form viable purposes of their own nor contribute to collective purposes, and if there is no cosmic purpose which makes this situation the best of all possible situations, human beings are indeed reduced to the helplessness of achieving nothing higher than awareness of their own futility.

However, the objection rests on the consequences of *humanist* assumptions, which exclude cosmic purpose and include the assumption that human beings are able to form and to fulfil purposes of their own on their own behalf, on behalf of others, on behalf of mankind, or together jointly. Does the fact of individual death and the probability of ultimate human extinction nullify such purposes? The actual fulfilment of purposes is a fact which cannot be nullified. Their value only is in question. But if human beings do in fact value achievements and enjoyments and their experience as such, is this really open to question? It is not open to question as a fact, but whether such enjoyments and evaluations have really given due weight to the fact of death and ultimate extinction is a question. If these facts are taken as inexorable and ultimate, as by humanists they are, do they not outweigh every other consideration? That is the force of the objection.

The answer turns on how far one is prepared to go in asserting that the temporal order of human existence is in itself an absolute frustration of human purposes and aspirations.

The temporal order

The vanity of human wishes is the age-old religious verdict on human behaviour, followed by the priestly sentence of non-attachment. This is because moth and rust corrupt and thieves break in and steal and everything is subject to time and chance. A man's reach should exceed this grasp. In Indian thought this meant purging the mind of its objects, the ultimate of non-attachment. Even the Greek or Roman sage, accepting the general verdict of experience, aimed at an unassailable serenity, either by schooled indifference to what happened or by restricting operations to the narrow limits within which wise choice and avoidance could be relied on to provide immunity. A modern unbeliever like the young Bertrand Russell accepts the diagnosis and borrows the remedy: a total resignation must be achieved by personal re-nunciation of all desired goods subject to time and chance. In this way the giants Fate, Death, Time,

Pain, and Despair are slain single-handed in one heroic encounter. The hero enjoys in a beatific vision the radiance of a new world of eternal things—the Past, Art, Knowlege, his own Ideals.

To seek to live beyond time and death is the last folly of noble souls. But what is the alternative, to snatch at the moments as they fly? Walter Pater in the Conclusion to *The Renaissance* gave an ideal to his disciples: to live in the informed, charged sensations of the moment, not in reflection.

> Not the fruit of experience, but experience itself, is the end. A counted number of pulses only is given to us of a variegated dramatic life. How may we see in them all that is to be seen in them by the finest senses? . . . With this sense of the splendour of our experience and of its awful brevity, gathering all we are into one desperate effort to see and touch, we shall hardly have time to make theories about the things we see and touch.

This may be just the thing for undergraduates, but like youth it is not a stuff that will endure. However, the strong accent on the present moment and the intense idealism of its cultivation are permanently needed correctives, and Pater does better justice to the permanence of his own ideal in *Marius the Epicurean*, in a passage at the end of chapter viii which sets cultivation of the present, and of the self for the present, in the context of 'a general completeness of life' governed by an acquired personal art guided by 'Insight'.

Life as the end of life in Pater's phrase, experience for its own sake, the finality and sufficiency of human values, this is the citadel of the humanist position. Is it defensible?

Time and Death, the capital human fears, devourers of all human hopes, the ravagers and spoilers, to be cheated, resisted, defied, by all devices, stratagems, and fortitudes in the armoury of heart and imagination, this is the capital mistake. For without time and death, no life and mind. Time and death are not forfeits, nor heavy weights in the balance against the little things, few or many, we manage to put into the other scale, nor even the primordial and inexorable conditions of all our enjoyments; they are, rather, present and actual utilities and resources necessary to all our values. As a painting is unthinkable apart from the surface on which it is laid out or a piece of music apart from the sequence of the notes which it is, so all our experience is not merely in time and space but is in the media of time and space; it is what it is by their indispensable means. If destruction as well as construction is bound up with the medium, that also is indispensable. 'Nor will any construction, however broadly based, have an *absolute* authority; the indomitable freedom of life to be more, to be new, to be what it has not entered into the heart of man as yet to conceive, must always remain standing. With that freedom goes the modesty of reason that can lay claim only to partial knowledge, and to the ordering of a particular soul, or city, or civilization' (Santayana: *Three Philosophical Poets*, p. 212).

This acceptance of time and destruction as essential human resources of life and living, instead of revolt against or submission to them

as the annihilating doom which poisons every
fruit of human energies, is part of the central
humanist recognition of the absolute and the
eternal as the enemy, since they spell Death and
Time with capitals, that is to say, they play the
roles of death and time in relation to human
possibilities not temporally but definitively, not
creatively/destructively   but   catastrophically:
the Deathless and Timeless are the truly lifeless
and finished. When the young Russell in the early
essay looked up from the midst of life's experiences to contemplate History and Art and Science
and Ideals as transcendental objects salvaged
from the wreck of human desires wrought by
Fate, Death, Time, Pain, Despair, he was really
looking away from life and death at Death in the
form of these absolutes: this free man's worship
was the worship of Death as the absolute in the
absolute. This is life for the sake of culture, instead
of culture for the sake of life, a vicious inheritance
from philosophy and theology.

The humanist aspires to use past, present,
and future, life and death, the arts and sciences,
ideas and ideals, along with all other resources,
as developing means of achieving the better
possibilities open to him. This is a very abstract
statement, but it covers a very concrete content,
since it represents the most sustained and systematic attempt to escape from the tyranny of
empty abstractions and to maximize the fertile
interplay of the ideal and the actual, past,
present, and future, culture and experience. The
humanist knows that he relies on the temporal
order for his life, for the power to learn from
experience, to draw on the past for standards and

means by which to enjoy the present and create the future.

Of course it would be quite absurd to pretend, or to allow oneself to assume, that time is always on the side of the best endeavour, that death comes only when wanted or needed or appropriate. There is an element of sheer ineliminable fatality obstructive to any human interest. We mourn: and are not comforted. The best laid schemes of mice and men require insurances, and there is no insurance: there is irreparable loss.

There are advantages and disadvantages both on humanist assumptions and on Christian assumptions. Which has the more favourable balance is a question worth raising, since it is perhaps generally assumed that there is no question here; but, for the humanist at any rate, the real comparison is of the evidence for the assumptions.

Because human life is temporal and remains a skein of possibilities, so long as it remains at all, it has no definitive character, and cannot be written up nor written down nor written off, neither in a literary manner as tragedy or epic or farce, nor in a scientific manner as a statistical assessment of probable pleasures and pains. Although there can be no justifiable general and abiding judgement on human life as a whole, each human life, as it completes itself, may be judged, from within and from without. The individual may find the circumstances of his personal life intolerable to him; he may decide to bring its pointlessness to an end. Anyone, as he gets to know about people's lives, may gather impressions that deepen with the years that human life as option is simply not worth taking up. It may be there is an indeterminable threshold below which life is nasty and brutish and would be better if also short.

These gloomy possibilities, which everybody knows are not figments, are of course offset by the splendid panorama from the summits of sublime moments. There is heaven and there is hell in the economy of every human imagination. It is best to avoid lurid colours and the rhetoric which takes the place of thought when people climb up for the grand view of human affairs. One sees only a small part of a moving picture, and it is not a film as others are. Therefore there is no sense in judging as if one stood in front of an easel.

Human beings in the midst of these possibilities for better and for worse which promise and menace, and for which they are responsible, need confidence, they need a boost. If this does not come from religious faith, it can come only from the available natural and human resources. Such resources are not themselves a vision that can create confidence, but they are resources which have inspired such visions in the past, and they have power to do so now. For the human being is more than himself and he has more than the present which he grasps. He may become deeply aware of the interpenetration of phases in his own life and in that of mankind. There is no present moment that is not charged with the past and pledged to the future. Within this imaginative grasp and this mortal span, I am the author of my own experience. That experience may be but a sorry or trivial tale of what happens to me. Or I may take it in hand and create an experience that is worth sharing, not for its moral but for itself. Such a creation requires an art of living which is the better part of civilization and, for the most part, is still to be learned, although its rudiments are familiar. Humanism is an aspiration to breed this confidence rooted in available resources and an attainable art, and thus to reduce the pointlessness of individual lives which exclaim against the pointlessness of it all. The answer to the objection is necessarily a practical one, and must be judged accordingly.

THE AUTHORS:

H. J. Blackham is Director of the newly formed British Humanist Association and Secretary of the Ethical Union.

Ronald Hepburn is Professor of Philosophy at the University of Nottingham.

Kingsley Martin was Editor of *The New Statesman* from 1931–60 and is now Editorial Director of the same paper.

Kathleen Nott, poetess, novelist and philosophic literary critic, is a frequent contributor to *The Observer*.